The official Dream Dinner Party Handbook

GARY M. ALMETER

HUMORIST BOOKS

New York

First Printing: 2022
ISBN 978-1-954158-12-2

Humorist Books is an imprint of *Weekly Humorist* owned and operated by Humorist Media LLC.

Weekly Humorist is a weekly humor publication, subscribe online at weeklyhumorist.com

110 Wall Street New York, NY 10005

weeklyhumorist.com - humoristbooks.com - humoristmedia.com

Edited by Andy Newton
Additional material written by Zoë Appelbaum and Lily Emalfarb
Cover, illustrations, and book design by Marty Dundics

Let's Get Ready!

You don't want to look like an idiot in front of your heroes!

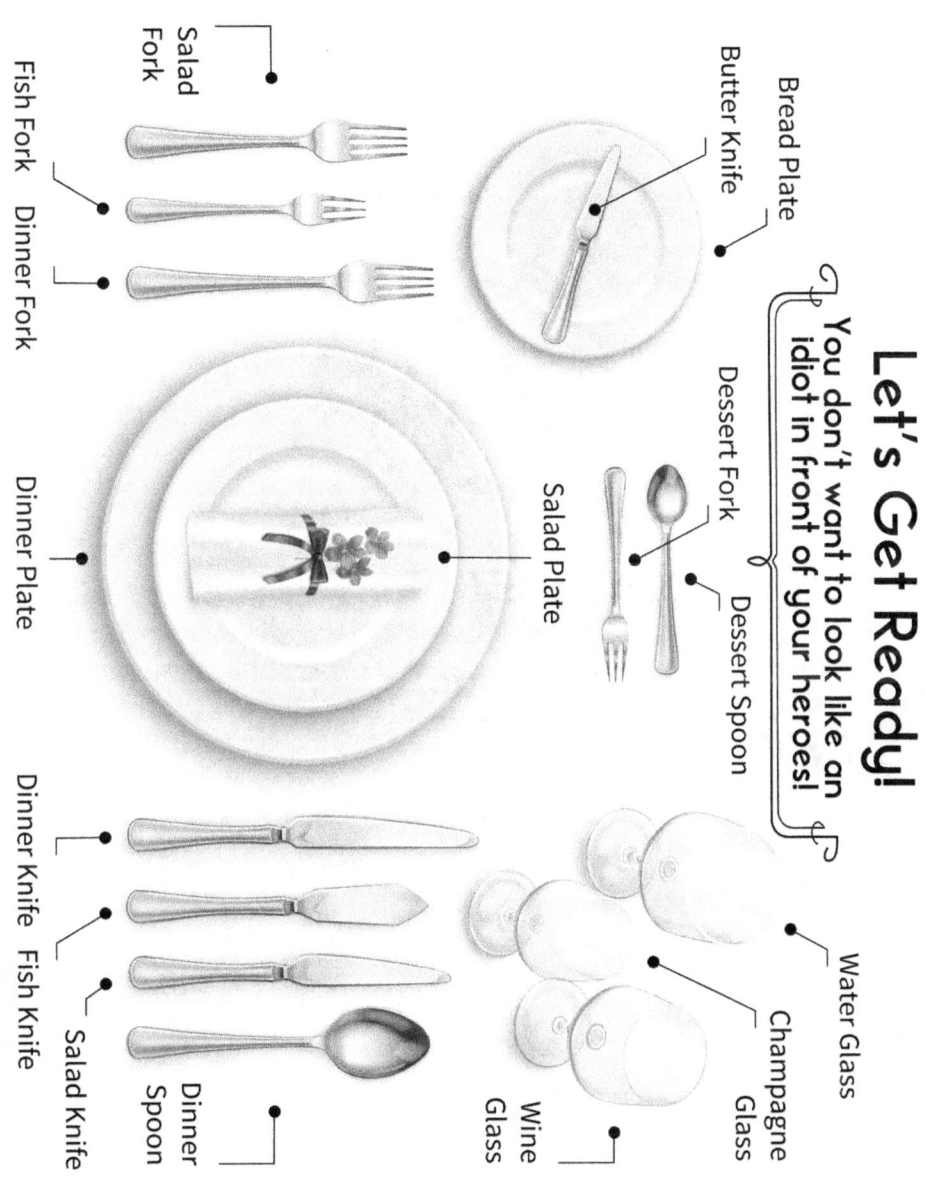

Salad Fork

Fish Fork   Dinner Fork

Butter Knife

Bread Plate

Dessert Fork

Dessert Spoon

Salad Plate

Dinner Plate

Dinner Knife   Fish Knife

Salad Knife

Dinner Spoon

Wine Glass

Champagne Glass

Water Glass

Introduction

I.   *Introduction*

The day for which you have been waiting, about which you have been asked, and about which you have been contemplating for decades, is approaching. Your dream dinner party is nigh. Yes, THAT dream dinner party. The one for which you get to choose three invitees, living or dead, and eat dinner with them. So many people to choose from! So many people vying for a place at your table: explorers, artists, singers, ancestors, presidents, authors, philosophers, religious leaders—anyone who has ever lived. It can be overwhelming. And you can't mess it up.

This book, the *official* dream dinner party handbook, is the only handbook you need (and you do need a handbook) to assist you in selecting the three invitees best suited for you.

The question, "Which three people, living or dead, would you invite to your dream dinner party?" is posed to us with some frequency: it's a general ice-breaking device; it's a frequent question in party games; it's a question posed in dating apps and is therefore somehow a key indicator of what kind of potential mate you will attract; it's a common college application essay question; and it's genuinely fun to think about.

I'm certain you have been asked who you might invite to your dream dinner party in some context. It was one of my college application essays. I'm ashamed to say that I do not even remember who I identified in my essay. I was neither very daring nor very confident when I was applying to colleges, an endeavor which inherently fosters obsequiousness and an eagerness to at least *appear* erudite. As such, I likely included Abraham Lincoln as a guest. And since all three of the colleges to which I applied were Catholic, I think it is likely that I included Mother Teresa of Calcutta. She was so hot in the 1980s, the Scarlett Johansson of the poor. You could scarcely leave your house without being inundated with Mother Teresa of Calcutta gossip. I applied to colleges at a time when U2 was also very hot, so I likely included Bono, as well, to suggest to the admissions people that there was also a creative, sensitive, social justice-y component to my person. Bono and Abraham Lincoln and Mother Teresa. What could go wrong?

I am delighted to say that I was accepted at all three colleges to which I applied and thusly, I am highly qualified to write this book. That said, if I am ever an admissions officer at a college and in response to the question, "What three people would you invite to your dream dinner party?" the applicant includes Mother Teresa of Calcutta, I will deny him or her admission instantly. Probably with a big rubber stamp that says "REJECTED" that I will pound into a red ink spongey thing and then pound on the paper with authority and disdain. Because wanting to share a meal with Mother Teresa of Calcutta is just stupid. More on her later.

Later, a friend of mine was selected to host his dream dinner party and he asked me to help him select his guests. I knocked it out of the park. He ended up with Tom Landry, Fyodor Dostoyevsky, and Billie Holiday. I've also successfully matched Jacqueline Kennedy, Frederick Douglass, and Pablo Picasso with a particularly demanding client who told me "she had the time of her life" and matched Che Guevara (the famous t-shirt guy), Cleopatra, and Sammy Davis, Jr. with a client who was on the cusp of making the biggest mistake of his life by inviting Elvis Presley, William Shakespeare, and George Washington. I've also successfully negotiated on behalf of clients to: make Queen Victoria and Prince Albert count as ONE dinner guest, prompt Jean-Michel Basquiat to make a painting that the host could KEEP, and negotiated an appearance by cool, *On the Waterfront* Marlon Brando when the host failed to specify which Marlon Brando she wanted and was about to get big crazy Marlon Brando. And while I rarely suggest inviting Elvis to a dream dinner party unless there are extenuating circumstances, I have saved many people from an evening with freebasing peanut butter in Graceland Elvis when they fail to specify that they want "Blue Hawaii" Elvis.

My methods work.

With all the focus on the question, then, it is likely that your dream dinner party is imminent. You have finally been tasked with conceptualizing, planning, orchestrating, and executing your dream dinner party. It had always been inevitable and is currently imminent. And it's something that will likely only happen one time. You only get one shot, do not miss this chance to blow this opportunity comes once in a lifetime. (See, Eminem, Chapter V). Let's do it right.

Because you have had decades to contemplate, ruminate, speculate, and excogitate on the invitees to your dream dinner party, you don't want to mess it up, squander the opportunity, and when asked, just blurt out the standards, "Abraham Lincoln and Jesus and Princess Diana." What a waste that would be. Like what would Jesus and Princess Diana even talk about? Can Princess Diana even speak Aramaic? You would spend your entire dream dinner party navigating

FUN FACT

This one time, Charo and Abraham Lincoln were at the same dream dinner party (don't ask), and Abe had a little bit too much to drink and accidentally put Charo's fruit basket on his head when it was time to go home. No one had the courage to say anything.

the tensions and brokering peace between Jesus and Princess Diana, who, and I don't like to gossip, could be quite a drama queen. Well not *quite* a queen but you know what I mean. And once peace was brokered, you'd have to spend the dessert course explaining the phenomenon of Princess Diana to Abraham Lincoln, who would likely be more interested in the state of his beloved United States than a princess. And what Abraham Lincoln are we getting at this dream dinner party? Illinois attorney Lincoln? Wood-chopping, walking-to-school-in-the-Kentucky-wilderness Lincoln? Post-Gettysburg-Address-euphoria Lincoln? Or post-assassination Abraham Lincoln? And if so, does he have a gaping head wound? Who wants to spend their dream dinner party addressing someone's gaping head wound? And how fun could a dinner with Jesus really be? The tenets of his signature work expressly prohibit indulgence. So that dessert course, assuming you haven't lost your appetite from Abraham Lincoln's gaping head wound and Princess Diana hasn't stormed out after getting dirty looks from Jesus, would be served with a heaping portion of guilt a la mode. And wouldn't Princess Diana be distracted throughout the evening asking questions like "Who's Kate Middleton?", "Who's Meghan Markle?", or "What do you mean Harry and Meghan have jettisoned the family?" She is not going to want to sit there and talk to you and Jesus when she could be canoodling with all of her (absolutely adorable!!!!) grandchildren.

So, let's invite that other staple, Shakespeare. That would be a ton of fun to listen to him talk about himself all night. And what if you want sushi at your dream dinner party? Would you have to teach Ferdinand Magellan how to use chopsticks? Yes? Forget it. So, let's invite Pope Francis. We'd need to invite an interpreter. And would that interpreter count as one of your dream dinner party guests? And what if Pope Francis decides he wants to wash everyone's feet? IS Abraham Lincoln even comfortable with that? We would likely need to invite an interpreter for Jesus, also. You know any good Aramaic interpreters? Would the Wright Brothers count as one guest or two? What about Lewis and Clark? Could you invite Hitler and kill him after dessert? Or kill him before dessert so he doesn't get to enjoy it? And what about that Lincoln conundrum? What if you invite someone who died a grisly death? Like, what if the cause of their demise was a decapitation? Do they come to your dinner party as sentient beings capable of communication but holding their head in their hands? Like, what if you have this thing for Marie Antoinette and you want her at your dream dinner party and you don't know if she will arrive as a fully functional human being or if she will be a body holding her head in her hands and the head will be moving its mouth. Would Lewis and Clark come to the party dressed in like their moose coats and coonskin caps? With muskrat dung and campfire gristle in their beards? That would be true to character—again, I do not like to gossip—but decidedly uncouth by most standards of etiquette.

With decades to have thought about this, you'd think you'd have given enough foresight to the prospect of muskrat dung and campfire gristle. What is wrong with you?

Can true-crime buffs just invite "the man known as Jack the Ripper," expect that man to show up, and then question him until they find out his true identity? This could serve the dual purpose of satiating one's own curiosity and creating an inevitable windfall when they reveal the identity of one of history's most notorious and notoriously unknown criminals.

It's best to establish these sorts of protocols at the outset before you waste a dream dinner party guest spot on Pope Francis's interpreter (or waste time filling his foot washing basin); or Orville, the lesser of the two Wright brothers, who is just as known for eating with his fingers as he is for half-inventing the airplane; or the Captain, who just played piano while Tennille sang the songs with those sweet buttery molasses and mascarpone vocals.

DREAM DINNER PARTY GUESTS WHO WOULD'VE LOVED CHIPOTLE, BUT WHOSE DEMISE OCCURRED BEFORE THEY COULD TASTE CHIPOTLE, SO IF YOU SERVED THEM CHIPOTLE AT YOUR DREAM DINNER PARTY, YOU'D REALLY ROCK THEIR AFTER-LIVES:

- Jacqueline Bouvier Kennedy Onassis
- Queen Elizabeth I
- Montezuma
- Johannes Brahms*
- Mark Twain
- Eleanor Roosevelt (obviously)
- Golda Meir
- Joan of Arc

* Brahms is identified on this list because just as he, along with Bach and Beethoven, was part of the three Bs of music, so too Chipotle has perfected the three Bs of Mexican food: beans, burritos, and barbacoa.

You hold in your hands the complete and official guide for planning your dream dinner party. When—and the day is surely nigh—it is time for you to plan your dream dinner party for real, you are going to be prepared.

We are all human beings with our own interests and baggage and needs and histories and aspirations. No two dream dinner party guest lists should be the same. Somewhere there is a woman holding this book in her hands, and this woman is an electrical engineer who plays tennis on weekends and loves *The Bell Jar*. Should she select Nikola Tesla, Serena Williams, and Sylvia Plath? Of course, she should. Unless she also hates being an electrical engineer and wants to retire. In which case, she might be better off inviting Vincent Van Gogh instead of Nikola Tesla, so while she's playing tennis with Serena and chatting with Sylvia between sets, Vincent can be painting something for her to sell when the dream dinner party concludes so that she can retire from his shitty electrical engineering job. Somewhere, holding this book, there's an architect who likes to sing showtunes in the shower and ice-skate. His list will likely include I.M Pei, Bette Midler (and/or Julie Andrews), and Adam Rippon. Or maybe he's struggling with his faith. In which case, invite Jesus to the dinner. Jesus and Bette Midler and Adam Rippon.

In the end, only *you* can decide who you invite to your dream dinner party. With this official guide, it's going to be the very best dream dinner party it can be!!

II. *Establish Goals*

Before delving into the decisions of your dream dinner party (*see* "Decisions, Decisions, Decisions") you will need to establish your goals for the dinner. Like some single-issue voters, some dream dinner party hosts yearn for one thing and one thing only, whether it's to have one last meal with a departed grandparent or to talk physics with Sir Isaac Newton or bake a croquembouche with Julia Child or try to return a serve from Arthur Ashe or merely be in the presence of Martin Luther King, Jr. A common error I see all too frequently is for a host to identify the one person who absolutely needs to be at your dream dinner party, identifying him or her, and treating the remaining dream dinner party guests after-thoughts. With some strategic forethought, even single-issue dream dinner party hosts can make all their dream dinner party guests meaningful.

To establish goals, you will first need to ascertain, from the one who has granted you the dream dinner party, how malleable your guests will be, or rather, how much control of your guests' behaviors you will have. For example, can you *require* a painter to paint something for you in between the salad and the entrée course? If so, then let's invite Mark Rothko, Vincent Van Gogh, and Leonardo da Vinci to the dream dinner party, invite (or command) them to collaborate on a large piece for you, then

EAT ME!

Vincent Van Gogh-nache

This is that thing of when you host a dinner party and make a swirly chocolate dessert with extra nuts!!

sell that at Sotheby's for about a billion dollars. Of course, this will also require some notice. You will need to go to the arts and crafts supply store and purchase some brushes and canvases and paints. Or if you're inviting Julia Child, you'll need time to go grocery shopping. It's pointless to invite Julia Child to a dream dinner party if you have nothing but Cheerios, milk, Tabasco sauce, a jar of olives, spaghetti, some American cheese slices in those plastic sleeves, those packets of teriyaki sauce you get from Chinese take-out and save in your drawer, eggs, and peanut butter in your home. Similarly, it'd be pointless to invite Coco Chanel to a dream dinner party and not have some black fabric, preferably a nice chenille and some tulle overlay, on hand for her to make you your own little black dress.

FUN

This is a perfectly valid goal for a dream dinner party. If you want to simply dine and converse and maybe play charades and then, after their allotted time with you, have your dream dinner party guests get celestially whisked back through the universe and/or afterlife to where they dwell, then have at it.

People's ideas of what constitutes fun are widely varied, so the universe of potential invitees is wide-open here. (Though, it's probably best to avoid the likes of Socrates and Mussolini and Ho Chi Minh and Mother Teresa.) Comedians would be fun. If you're into poker, then invite the world's top poker players for a fun game of Texas Hold 'Em. If you're into chess, invite Bobby Fischer. But be aware that Bobby Fischer is a notorious recluse. Same analysis for avid players of Scrabble, Monopoly, pool, cornhole, baseball, ping pong, etc.

Fun also necessarily encompasses deceased friends and siblings and other playmates. Let's assume that sexual intercourse is not an option for any dream dinner party scenario, as there's something sort of creepy about inviting someone to a dream dinner party and assuming they will have sex with you. But remember that special friend you had who was taken too soon when he chased that paper boat into the sewer and got eaten by that mean clown? Inviting him to a dream dinner party so you can play hopscotch together one last time before he goes back to the nether world would be very fun.

What else is fun? If all things *Facts of Life* is your idea of fun, then invite Lisa Whelchel, Mindy Cohn, and Kim Fields, a.k.a. Blair, Natalie, and Tutti from *The Facts of Life*. You can either be Jo or Mrs. Garrett, and you can spend your dream dinner party reenacting scenes from the hit NBC show. That sounds like so much fun. That goes for any movie and TV show. If sailing is your idea of fun, then invite John Paul Jones, William Bligh, and Ferdinand Magellan, and if able, hold your dream dinner party on a boat.

Many of our respondents, because we are all human beings, identified Marilyn Monroe as a dream dinner party guest. Some just to meet her, some to ask her specific questions, and some to engage in intimacy with her. Intimacy is fun, but is it permitted? Generally, no. Because it's weird and creepy to invite someone to dinner and expect to engage in intimacy with them. And it's rude. What will other guests be doing while you and Marilyn Monroe or Cary Grant or Wilt Chamberlain or Heidi Klum or Abraham Lincoln are engaging in the intimacy?

General Knowledge

If you just want to learn something, then invite history's great thinkers to dine with you, where they will inevitably enlighten you with their knowledge.

There are different types of knowledge. There is general knowledge that exists purely to enlighten. There is familial/ancestral knowledge; there is knowledge specific to an occupation, or knowledge you need to strike it rich. If you just want to spend an evening listening and ruminating and postulating, then

PRO TIP

George Washington will arrive 15 minutes early and usually arrives empty-handed. Better to invite Alexander Hamilton, who is still definitely having a moment.

invite the likes of Confucius, Plato, Aristotle, Jesus, and the like to offer wisdom, self-improvement tips, general principles of the human condition, and general tenets of living well.

The level and degrees of knowledge can be tailored. If you're eager to find out the process that went into writing the United States Constitution and the general tenor of the Constitutional Convention of 1787, then invite George Washington, James Madison, and Alexander Hamilton. Play the Soundtrack for *Hamilton* during dinner and explain rap to the real Alexander Hamilton. Or remove James Madison and invite Lin Manuel-Miranda in his stead to give it a whole different feel. Ask them, "What is the deal with the 2nd amendment anyway?" Want to know what it was like to walk on the moon? Then invite Neil Armstrong. Dying to know what it was like at Appomattox Courthouse? Invite Ulysses S. Grant and Robert E. Lee. Grant and Lee would be all, "the food at Appomattox courthouse was so bland" and "remember that dress Mrs. Lincoln wore – have you ever?" so a third guest

FOR ALL YOU PHILISTINES...

As of 2020, a total of twelve men* have walked on the moon:

- Neil Armstrong, Apollo 11, 1969
- Buzz Aldrin, Apollo 11, 1969
- Pete Conrad, Apollo 12, 1969
- Alan Bean, Apollo 12, 1969
- Alan Shepard, Apollo 14, 1971
- Edgar Mitchell, Apollo 14, 1971
- David Scott, Apollo 15, 1971
- John Young, Apollo 16, 1972
- Charles Duke, Apollo 16, 1972
- Gene Cernan, Apollo 17, 1972
- Harrison Schmitt, Apollo 17, 1972.

* A woman has yet to walk on the moon. This even though a woman named Margaret Hamilton wrote the computer code for the first moon landing. To say nothing of the contributions of the "hidden figures" ladies, Katherine Johnson, Dorothy Vaughn, and Mary Jackson.

* Apollo 13 was supposed to land on the moon, but because an oxygen tank exploded on the craft's service module, the crew had to abandon their mission and a spectacular recovery ensued. You can watch the Kevin Bacon and Bill Paxton movie called *Apollo 13* for more information.

would take some creative thinking. But if you're that into the Civil War, you'll likely think of someone.

Occupational Knowledge

More specific knowledge comes from experts in a particular field. If you are a French chef, there could be nothing better than inviting Julia Child to your dream dinner party and cook with her. Want to improve your back stroke? Invite Michael Phelps. Want to learn the general principles of restraint in the face of injustice? Then invite Barack Obama. Lawyers, doctors, race car drivers, carpenters, architects, IT people, event planners, fashion designers, engineers, chemists, economists, etc.

Wealth

Warren Buffett narrowly missed our Top Ten. Presumably people want him at their dream dinner party so he can dispense complementary investment advice. Which assumes that he would dispense complimentary investment advice at your dream dinner party. And that doesn't sound too fun. Or memorable. It's like you're spending your dream dinner party watching an episode of CNBC's "Squawk Box". A highly intimate, up-close-and-personal episode of "Squawk Box," but an episode of "Squawk Box" nonetheless.

If wealth is the primary goal of your dream dinner party, and I'm not saying it should or should not be, then at least make it interesting. Imagine the money you could make from inviting John Lennon, Paul McCartney, and George Harrison (and Ringo Starr if you're permitted a fourth) to your dream dinner party, inviting them to sing this new song you wrote, recording that singing, and then selling it. But do you want to spend your dream dinner party time cajoling the Beatles to sing a song you wrote for them? Or fiddling with microphones and extension cords and recording equipment?

Typically, anything your guests create can and will be metaphysically left behind upon their departure. Like, if you invite Georgia O'Keeffe to your dream dinner party and you ask her to paint you something and she does and then she returns to her celestial resting place, the painting remains. So invite Andy Warhol and ask him to paint you something and then sell it at auction. Invite Anita O'Day or Frank Sinatra to your dream dinner party, invite them to sing something you've written, record it and then sell it. Authenticating these things can be problematic so you'll need to identify someone willing and able to authenticate

Another avenue for turning your dream dinner party into a money-making venture is to invite dream dinner party guests who can solve mysteries for you. Ask Leonardo da Vinci the identity of the model for the Mona Lisa. You could also ask him to paint something for you after dessert. Invite Lee Harvey Oswald and ask him if he acted alone. I mean, who is a better judge of character than you? No one. You totally knew that your sister's new boyfriend Chad was going to be a total disaster and leave her life in ruins and make wretched her destiny. Right? You will be able to tell if Lee Harvey Oswald is lying. You totally will. Invite Jimmy Hoffa and ask him where he is buried. Invite Lizzie Borden and ask her if she really murdered her father and step-mother. Should you be inclined, you might also invite unidentified and otherwise unidentifiable historical figures like Jack the Ripper, and when they appear, ask them, "Who are you?" The feasibility of this depends on the omnipotence of the individual orchestrating the dream dinner party. Typically, those orchestrating dream dinner parties are omnipotent, so if you say, I want "the man known as D.B. Cooper, the man known as Jack the Ripper, and the lady known as the Babushka Lady on the Grassy Knoll" and when they appear at your table, politely ask, "What is your real name?" Other possibilities include the sailor and the girl in the V-J Day parade photo, the Last Jew in Vinnitsa, Banksy, or Zodiac Killer (even though we all know the Zodiac Killer is Ted Cruz). The availability of incontrovertible proof varies for each of these, so do determine the level of incontrovertibility before banking on a post-dream dinner party windfall.

Ancestral Connection / Familial Reconnection

A sizable number of respondents identified deceased relatives, both known and unknown, as potential dream dinner party guests. I advise against doing this for several reasons.

The recent availability of genealogy research tools and genetic analysis has fostered a renewed interest teetering on preoccupation with one's ancestors. It might be tempting to invite the great-great-grandparent who emigrated from his or her country of origin or the ancestor for whom all information is missing (or deleted!) in the Anestry.com database or the ancestor who fought in the Revolutionary War or Civil War or engaged in or experienced some event of historical significance. Inviting a great grandparent or great-great-grandparent or some other such unknown ancestor just to "see what he or she is like" would satisfy curiosity, but there is also the possibility that you discover that he or she is a loathsome individual. This is known in dream dinner party parlance as the "Confederate Uncle or Nazi Kinfolk" phenomenon, or CUNK. You don't want to get CUNKed at your own dream dinner party. This will have a corrosive effect on your self-esteem. Unless there is something sufficiently interesting or significant about an ancestor, stick to famous people.

Second, inviting a deceased relative or friend that you knew will invariably have some unintended and unforeseeable consequences. It would be impossible to accurately predict what sort of effect inviting your great-great-grandfather to the dream dinner party might have. And to those deceased relatives who you knew, inviting them to the dream dinner party would necessarily mean you would have to say goodbye to them again. Would this mean having to go through the stages of grief all over again? It might. While research is all over the place with this, only you know your emotional bandwidth for dining with a deceased loved one. Obviously, you must weigh the threat of renewed grief against the benefit of being able to relay messages to the descendant that you weren't able to prior to their demise. This could be cathartic. Lastly, the joy generated by inviting a deceased grandparent or sibling or parent to a dream dinner party would be tempered by the resentment of those you did not invite. For example, say you invite Grandma, Abraham Lincoln, and John Lennon to your dream dinner party. You finish dessert, they go back to from whence they came, and you call you sister to tell her that you just had a dream dinner party with Grandma. Do you think that she'll be happy you invited John Lennon instead of her to the dream dinner party? Spoiler alert: she won't be happy you invited John Lennon to your dream dinner party to hang with grandma and not her. It's the curse of the lottery winner who, for the rest of his or her life, will be criticized for never giving enough money at every wedding, birthday party, bar mitzvah, and fundraising dinner to which he or she is invited.

Those who shared a special bond with a deceased relative will surely want him or her there. Typically, we have found that this adds additional stressors to the dream dinner party. Like, how do you divide your time between your beloved deceased grandmother and Robert E. Lee? Or what if your great-grandmother wants to get all cozy with Robert E Lee? Talk about a double-CUNK! Or how does the great-grandfather who was more into blacksmithing than wordsmithing break bread with Virginia Woolf or Ernest Hemingway? The good news is that our research has found that people are quite open to new ideas. Once you explain to your great grandfather that women wear pants now, curse, and generally don't like to be called "babe" or "toots" he will surprise you with how quickly he can acclimate. Same with people of different ethnicities and backgrounds. Invite Jane Goodall and do an experiment on how people are inherently inclined to accept others when not watching Fox News. Invite George Washington and Pete and Chasten Buttigieg and see how quickly conversation quickly turns to the state of American infrastructure and transportation methods once George digests that men can marry one another. Invite George Washington and Ted Cruz and Lauren Boebert and see how quickly George leaves the dinner in disgust.

Greater synergy happens when the deceased relative and the dream dinner party host have a common interest. Like, a dream dinner party host and a deceased grandmother with a mutual love for the Green Bay Packers would naturally invite Vince Lombardi as a dream dinner party guest. Similarly, it makes sense for a dream dinner party host and a deceased grandfather with a shared love for old movies to invite Katherine Hepburn or Hen-

FOR ALL YOU PHILISTINES...

Most iconic dresses of all time:

- Audrey Hepburn's little black dress from *Breakfast at Tiffany's*
- Beyonce's 2015 Riccardo Tisci for Givenchy Met Gala Dress
- Princess Diana's 1994 little black "revenge" dress
- Diane von Furstenberg's wrap dress
- Elizabeth Taylor's gold *Cleopatra* dress
- Grace Kelly's blue dress from *To Catch a Thief*
- Jackie Kennedy's peach satin Oleg Cassini dress she wore to India
- Jennifer Lopez's 2000 Grammy Awards Versace dress
- Marilyn Monroe's *Seven Year Itch* top of the subway grate halter dress
- Michelle Obama's 2009 Inaugural gown designed by Jason Wu
- Tina Turner's metallic gold flapper dress
- Bjork's 2001 Academy Awards swan dress
- Coco Chanel's little black dress

ry Fonda or John Wayne to the dream dinner party. Or one of those grandmas who worked as a seamstress in New York City's fashion district in the 1920's dining with Coco Chanel. Though, keep in mind that if Coco Chanel is one of your dream dinner party guests and she is chit chatting with your great-grandma about sewing, then that is less time that she can spend making you that original Chanel little black dress we discussed earlier.

If you have some sort of unfinished business with a relative, the dream dinner party is not the occasion at which to address it. Why waste a spot at the dream dinner party just to accost some poor dead great-aunt about who went to the grave (falsely) believing that her potato salad was creamier and zestier than yours?

If your life will not be complete without reconnecting with some ancestor or relative, known or unknown, invite someone else in your family with whom that invitee also has a connection along with a famous person who can provide some other benefit. This will create a true family atmosphere, and your relative will have someone with whom to speak while you converse with a famous person of your choosing. You do not want to feel guilty at your dream dinner party for not paying enough attention to one of your guests.

Experience

Want to try to get a hit off Satchel Paige or strike out Jackie Robinson? Or play golf with Babe Didrikson Zaharias? Or return a serve from Serena Williams? Or see what happens when Nolan Ryan pitches to Babe Ruth? Or when Sir Isaac Newton discusses gravity and energy with Albert Einstein? Or when Rothko and Pollack have an "abstract expressionism-off"? Or when Alfred Hitchcock, Wes Craven, and Stephen King attempt to out-frighten each other? Then invite them to your dream dinner party! But first, confirm that you can dictate the behaviors of your guests. Babe Ruth was infamously stubborn. Telling him to "go bat" before he is done with the all-you-can-eat buffet might be an issue. And be sure that you can choose the location for your dream dinner party. Inviting Babe Ruth to bat against Nolan Ryan when there's no baseball diamond nearby will squelch the intended purpose of the dream dinner party. Same with having an Arnold Palmer with Arnold Palmer, Jack Nicklaus, and Tiger Woods at Augusta National Golf Club. Or playing soccer with Pele, Lionel Messi, and Cristiano Ronaldo. Or catching passes from Tom Brady, Peyton Manning, and Roger Staubach. Or playing tennis with Serena Williams, Martina Navratilova, and Billie Jean King. These possibilities are endless. Whatever and whomever you are into will dictate this, and I am delighted to say that there really are no wrong answers here.

Acceptance

If the goal of the dream dinner party is to garner acceptance at a college or graduate school or highly selective club whose initiation protocols include, in addition to a membership fee and appropriate pedigree, a proper answer to the dream dinner party question, then by all means select someone who will impress the decisionmakers. Anyone applying to Wharton should choose Andrew Carnegie, John D Rockefeller, and Marcus Goldman, and/or his son-in-law, Samuel Sachs, depending of course on if notable duos count as one guest or two. If pairs count as one in this context, you could invite Marcus Goldman and his son-in-law Samuel Sachs, Messrs. Smith and Barney, and both of the Lehman brothers!!! Oh, what fun that would be!!! A Wharton applicant should absolutely not identify Andy Warhol, Mark Rothko, and Pablo Picasso as his or her dream dinner party guests, unless of course the applicant can make a cogent argument that inviting those three, supplying them with canvases and paints, and then selling them is a sound—perhaps the *soundest*—investment. An Embry-Riddle applicant will of course want to include Chuck Yeager, Neil Armstrong, and at least one of the Wright Brothers.

If you seek a more general sort of acceptance, like you want to be deemed sophisticated and erudite by a certain crowd, then I suggest a simple tactic. First, identify three dream dinner party guests. They can be people with whom you really want to dine, but if you're more into gaining acceptance, then think of some smart people. Soren Kierkegaard is always a good one. As are Jean-Paul Sartre, Jane Goodall, B.F. Skinner, Stephen Hawking, Noam Chomsky, and Albert Camus. Just think of people you've heard smart people talk about. Then— and here's the trick—you just ask a question after you identify your invitees. Here, watch what I do: "Who would I invite to my dream dinner party? Gosh. Just off the top of my head, probably Sigmund Freud, Immanuel Kant,

and Margaret Mead! Can you imagine the arguments we would have?" *Et voila*! You are a smart person. In reality, the only argument I would have with Sigmund Freud, Immanuel Kant, and Margaret Mead is whether the burgers are done. That's it. That's the only argument I would have with them. But in asking the listener to think of the arguments we would have, the onus is on them. And you walk away with everyone thinking that you are composing arguments to have with Freud, Kant, and Mead. It sort of works with anyone. Just ask an erudite question teeming with incomprehensibility.

Love

The question—along with height, weight, eye color, hair color, children, marital status, education level, income, occupation, sexual preferences, age, favorite movies, what your friends would say about you, where you grew up, what your hopes for the future are—of what three people living or dead you would choose to have at your dream dinner party is a dating app staple. If you are looking for love on such an app, then selecting these dream dinner party guests can take on a new, rose-colored hue. Be careful who you select. You want to be honest, but you also don't want to repel potential suitors with too much honesty. If you yearn to dine with David Duke and you say so in your dating app profile, your potential mates will be more limited. And likely more fueled by hate.

Evergreen

How timeless do you want this dream dinner party to be? As I write this, Ukrainian president Volodymyr Zelenskyy is really hot right now. If I were to conduct my highly scientific poll of dream dinner party guests today, there is little doubt that he would appear on most people's lists. Something to do with the cerebral cortex and the hippocampus and the formation of memory. Clarence and Ginni Thomas are having a moment for different reasons. Having dinner with Dr. Anthony Fauci a couple years ago would have been a great get but having dinner with him *now* would be sort of so 2020. Who knows what a great get might be next year. It's just human nature to want to be hot right now. It is up to you to weigh the personal importance of being hot right now versus satisfying more long-term aspirations.

WHAT YOU'RE SAYING TO POTENTIAL SUITORS WHEN YOU SELECT CERTAIN DREAM DINNER PARTY GUESTS

- Abraham Lincoln: Unless you're revolting and/or vomit on me, you can expect sex on the first date.

- Vincent Van Gogh: We are having sex on the first date, and it's going to be wild.

- Mother Teresa: You can expect anal on the first date, regardless of how revolting you might be.

- Jesus: Do not expect sex on the first date or the second date or the third date or any date until we wed.

- Tom Hanks: No sex on the first date but lots of hugs and laughs.

- Barack Obama: Expect good sex on the first date.

- Elon Musk: Expect sex on the first date, but know that sex will be poor due to my sub-average genitalia.

- Gandhi: Expect the best sex of your life on the first date, but only after we weave a love-making cloak with hand-spun cotton.

- Shakespeare: Expect sex before the first date.

- Elvis: Expect sex on the first date, but my breath smells like peanut butter and bananas.

- John Lennon: Expect sex on the first date, but I have never ever 'scaped my genital area, so good luck.

- Albert Einstein: $E=mc^{69}$, if you know what I mean.

- Georgia O'Keeffe: I yearn to sex with a cougar.

- Lucille Ball: Expect sex on the first date, and expect to laugh.

I chose a date at random, Tuesday, August 3, 1954 and looked at the front page of the New York Times. On that day, the people who were "hot right now" were Guatemalan President Carlos Castillo Armas, Oregon Senator Wayne Morse, and Brigadier General Herbert Vogel. People who selected those three as dream dinner party guests, falling prey to their eagerness to be hot right now, likely were hot for a while, but might have developed some regrets about their dream dinner party selections later on.

III.   Details, Details, Details

The emphasis on the dream dinner is rightfully placed on who is there. And the guests will likely dictate the sort of dinner you will have. You do not want Mother Teresa to feel ill at ease in an opulent setting with crystal goblets and crystal plates and crystal forks. Additionally, since Mother Teresa was only five feet tall and hunched over most of the time, you will likely need a booster seat for her. Will booster seats be available at your dream dinner party? That is something you will need to clarify before you select your dream dinner party guests.

Location, Location, Location (and why am I saying everything thrice)

You can have dinner wherever you want. Adhering to a few cardinal rules will maximize the impact of your dream dinner party.

Should you host it yourself?

Some people's interpretation of the "dream" modifier in dream dinner party necessarily incorporates and includes a workless, task-less, stress-free dinner party. For others, hosting a dream dinner party means preparing everything **for** your guests. Only you know where you fall on this scale.

There are degrees of worklessness. For the homeowner eager to show off his or her home—perhaps you have a kitchen backsplash inspired by the Frida Kahlo's "Self Portrait With Thorn Necklace and Hummingbird" and you really want to show it to her; or you want to show Adam and Eve your own Garden of Eden (though be certain to ascertain if they are one guest or two); or you want Jackson Pollack to paint your dining room. You don't have to be a homeowner. You can be an apartment-dweller eager to spend his or her dream dinner party in a more casual setting, envisioning a more casual affair, lounging in sweats and a comfy sweatshirt.

There are those too who would revel in the challenge of cooking spaghetti for Frank Sinatra or New England clam chowder for John F. Kennedy, or the thrill and gratification that comes from lacing some Bosnian bean soup with cyanide before serving it to Gavrilo Princip in an effort to prevent WWI? Though in this scenario, you'd just be killing the man who assassinated Archduke Franz Ferdinand just for fun; which would likely have greater consequences for your mortal soul than if you served him cyanide laced Bosnian bean soup *before* he shot Franz Ferdinand.

If you are planning the ultimate "this will determine who the best basketball player of all time is" basketball game between Michael Jordan and LeBron James make sure you have access to a basketball court. Same with a tennis match between Serena Williams and Martina Navratilova or a golf match between Tiger Woods and Arnold Palmer.

Picnic/Outdoors

What the fuck is wrong with you? No, your dream dinner party should definitely not be a picnic or any traditional outdoor setting, including the heralded garden patio. Do you want to subject Thomas Jefferson to an afternoon of swatting flies? Can you imagine if one of your dream dinner party guests is allergic to bees (like Britney Spears) and gets stung by a bee and must leave? Even if you bring the EpiPen, you will have to plunge it into her thigh, and that would just be disruptive. Of course, if you can establish at the outset that deceased dream dinner party guests would be immune from any of the afflictions which ailed them during their earthly lifetimes.

Some frequent guests are notable because of where they are from. Truman Capote, for example. You want to see Truman Capote in his pre-metropolitan natural habitat? Then you'll be dining in Monroeville, Alabama and likely on a picnic blanket in the town square. Same with Marilyn Monroe. And anyone born before 1920.

If you are permitted to choose the location of your dream dinner party, without limitation, and if that location is paramount to the success and enjoyment of your dream dinner party, then an out-of-doors dream dinner party is permissible. For example, if Sir Edmund Hillary is

FUN FACT

In lieu of traditional pepperoni, Teddy Roosevelt liked to put his own cured meat on his pizzas. His favorite? Sausage he made from possums he used to shoot on the White House lawn.

on your dream dinner party guest list, it only makes sense for you to have that dream dinner party at Mt. Everest's summit. Though, good luck if Mother Teresa of Calcutta is also on your dream dinner party guest list because her teeny-weeny itty-bitty little bony body would surely blow away at the top of Mt. Everest. Unless your goal is watch Mother Teresa get blown away from the top of Mount Everest. To each their own. And yeah, a dream dinner party with Sir Edmund Hillary, Mother Teresa, and Julie Andrews circa *The Sound of Music* who can sing "The hills are alive with the sound of music...." atop Mt. Everest as Mother Teresa gets swooped away and carried away like an old plastic Target bag swirling around a Target parking lot on a cold windy January afternoon. I'd be into that.

Dining with Jefferson, Washington, Lincoln, and Roosevelt at the foot of Mount Rushmore would also be very interesting. And it doesn't have to be a Mount. You could have a dream dinner party with Babe Ruth at home plate of the new Yankee Stadium in Bronx, NY, or with Arthur Ashe as your guest at Arthur Ashe Stadium, home of the U.S. Open in Queens, NY. You could dine at Kitty Hawk with Wilbur and/or Orville Wright or at the Globe Theatre with Shakespeare.

You also needn't be tethered to the notion that you have to dine at a locale which is a monument to or site of the accomplishments of one of your guests. You could dine with Kurt Cobain on the Amalfi Coast or Robert E. Lee in Santorini, if you're so inclined.

Restaurant

If you determine that someone needs to cook the meal for your dream dinner party, and food will not simply appear along with your dream dinner party guests, then by all means have your dream dinner party at a restaurant. First, identify any restrictions. Can you be whisked away to "any cozy bistro in Paris" or "sushi in Tokyo at Sukiyabashi Jiro" or "a place with good steak"? If so, then determine what would suit you and your guests. You don't want to have to explain to George Washington what pizza is, nor do you want to listen to Mother Teresa whine about how the entrée you just got could feed a family in a third world country for weeks.

Paris? New York? Rome? Tokyo?

Since you can host your dream dinner party anywhere, it may seem like a no-brainer to double-dip and hold your dream dinner party at an exotic locale unrelated to the guests' origins or histories, just to also see an exotic locale. This is inadvisable. The location, rather than augmenting the dream dinner party, will distract you and your guests. Should you have three hours of dream dinner party, you will be tempted to spend two of those hours chatting with Shakespeare, Frank Sinatra, and Prince, and an hour touring Paris.

If, however, the dream dinner party grantor's concept necessarily includes a dream locale, and if there is no geographical factor related to any of your guests immediately manifests itself, then by all means go nuts and select a location that will be dream-like but not distracting.

Menu

What to serve? Can you only serve one thing? And let's say you want to make it something simple, like pizza, so you don't waste time talking about the food. Would you have to teach Jesus how to eat pizza? What about George Washington? Didn't George Washington have wooden teeth? Should you have smoothies on hand if George Washington is an invitee and shows up with his wooden teeth? Our dream dinner party concept necessarily means that you serve your favorite food without deleterious effects on your guests. This is your dream dinner party, so you should be able to eat what you want, right? Select menu items that you enjoy. This has the same sort of significance as the last meal served to death row inmates. And if you have to teach how to use chopsticks, then so be it. Pureeing ribs for George Washington might require a few more small kitchen appliances.

The best approach here is to select menu items you enjoy and which generally aren't deemed too offensive. Presumably, you will have some idea of whether or not any of your guests are vegetarians or vegans. Since all vegetarians and vegans talk about is the fact that they are vegetarians and vegans. And as mentioned above, having to explain Subway or sushi or Stevia to Abraham Lincoln will cut into your dream dinner party time and make Abraham Lincoln feel self-conscious.

FOR ALL YOU PHILISTINES...

The 25 best restaurants in the world:

- Mirazur, Menton, France
- Noma, Copenhagen, Denmark
- Asador Etxebarri, Axpe, Spain
- Gaggan, Bangkok, Thailand
- Geranium, Copenhagen, Denmark
- Central, Lima, Peru
- Mugaritz, San Sebastian, Spain
- Arpege, Paris, France
- Disfrutar, Barcelona, Spain
- Maido, Lima, Peru
- Den, Tokyo, Japan
- Pujol, Mexico City, Mexico
- White Rabbit, Moscow, Russia
- Azurmendi, Larrabetzu, Spain
- Septime, Paris, France
- Alain Ducasse Au Plaza, Paris, France
- Steirereck, Vienna Austria
- Odette, Singapore
- Twins Garden, Moscow, Russia
- Tickets, Barcelona, Spain
- Frantzen, Stockholm, Sweden
- Narisawa, Tokyo, Japan
- Cosme, New York, USA
- Quintonil, Mexico City, Mexico
- Alleno Paris Au Pavillon Ledoyen, Paris, France

FUN FACT

George Washington, in fact, didn't have wooden teeth. But by the time he was first inaugurated as president, he only had one of his natural teeth left. Denture issues plagued him his entire life, and his teeth consisted of a host of various material, like hippopotamus ivory, human teeth, and metal fasteners. He also had smallpox at one point, which left huge pock marks in his face. *Bon appétit!*

The real challenge here is identifying foods that won't offend the spiritually enlightened. Typically, one's level of spiritual enlightenment is directly proportional to one's disdain for excess. More succinctly, those who are authentically spiritually inclined tend not to gorge themselves. Perhaps identifying this as a potential problem is superfluous since those seeking to invite Jesus, Siddhartha Gautama, or Mahatma Gandhi to a dream dinner party are not one prone to excess anyway. But it is something of which you should be mindful. Like, you don't want to serve caviar at your dream dinner party only to have Paul the Apostle say "an ounce of this would feed a family in Africa for a year."

I say "authentically spiritually" because there is a subset of "spiritual leaders" who, if invited to your dream dinner party, will have no problem engaging in excess, to wit, Jerry Falwell, Jr., Jim Bakker, Joel Osteen, and anyone else you typically see on TV talking about how Christian they are. Though, if you invite any of those clowns to your dream dinner party, you have bigger problems than what to feed them. You will want to hide your valuables, if they are coming to your house. You want a chart of the shittiest televangelists in the world? Here it is: #1 All of them. They are all so shitty.

Also, if Shakespeare is there, and I am not suggesting he need be, then you are going to want to watch what you serve, lest you encourage him to do quotations. For example, you don't want to serve cakes and ale or you'll get shit like the following:

"Do you think because you are virtuous, that there shall be no more cakes and ale?"

Othello: Act 2, Scene 3.

Not planning to serve cakes or ale? You also won't be able to serve anything with garlic or cheese in it or you'll hear the following:

"O, he is as tedious as a tired horse, a railing wife; worse than a smokey house: I had rather live with cheese and garlic in a windmil, far, than than feed on cates and have him talk to me in any summer-house in Christendom."

Henry IV: Act 3, Scene 1

Or strawberries:

"My lord of Ely, when I was last in Holborn I saw good strawberries in your garden there; I do beseech you send for some of them."

Richard III: Act 3, Scene 4.

And you get the idea. Shakespeare is probably going to be a pain in the ass no matter what you serve. But if you must have him as a guest at your dream dinner party, and I am not suggesting you should, then be mindful of what you serve so you're not unwittingly encouraging him to quote himself.

Music

Music is a great way to create ambience. And it can foster dialogue during a dream dinner lull. But selecting the right music will be key to a successful dream dinner party. You can't have the Buddha freaking out when he hears an electric guitar.

The stereo system and general audio-visual capabilities of whatever room you're in will determine if and what music you have at your dream dinner party. If you're inviting a musician, and if you can control the guests, then you can just invite the guest to pay and sing his or her own music. Again, it would make no sense to invite Chopin to your dream dinner party for the purpose of playing music without a piano on premises. You also don't want to play something so foreign sounding that Abraham Lincoln will think it's coming from outer space. Like, imagine explaining to Bjork to Abraham Lincoln.

The biggest concern is if one of your dream dinner party guests is a musician. Then you are tasked with finding music that will not offend his or her sensibilities. You might be tempted to play Frank Sinatra, if Frank Sinatra is a guest at your dream dinner party. This is inadvisable. Why would you do this? Frank Sinatra might be flattered; or he might be annoyed at your obsequiousness. Frank does not seem like the type who would tolerate obsequiousness. The tough part of this is that if you love Frank Sinatra enough to invite him to your dream dinner party, then it stands to reason that he is one of your favorites and that his music is necessary to make your dream dinner party perfect. But dining with Sinatra and listening to Sinatra are two different things.

You obviously want to avoid offending a dream dinner party guest by playing the music of a rival, musical or otherwise. Though hearing what Beyonce thinks of Lizzo could be fun. Or vice versa.

Furniture/Appliances

As mentioned above, Mother Teresa will likely need a booster seat. Make sure there is a booster seat available should Mother Teresa be invited to your dream dinner party. Which she won't be because you are reading this awesome book.

Otherwise, there are really no restrictions when it comes to furniture. The degree to which you have to explain the purpose and/or function of furniture will depend on who you invite. You will have to explain what a table and chairs are if you invite some sort of Cro-Magnon man to your dream dinner party. I don't know any Cro-Magnon men or women by name. Presumably, you could just say "a representative Cro-Magnon man," and you will get one. I suspect that you would have to demonstrate how to use a La-Z-Boy recliner to Abraham Lincoln; or anyone born before La-Z-Boy recliners were invented. You also don't want guests to freak out when you start your blender, pureeing a sandwich or slice of pizza for one of the presidents who had wooden teeth.

Décor

Are any of your dream dinner party guests allergic to hydrangea? Will a centerpiece with LED lights confuse and/or frighten a dream dinner party guest from another century? Would a tablescape evoking national pride offend a dream dinner party guest from another country?

FOR ALL YOU PHILISTINES...

Big musical feuds:

- Prince v. Michael Jackson
- Nicki Minaj v. Miley Cyrus
- Taylor Swift v. Katy Perry
- Whitney Houston v. Mariah Carey
- Brian Wilson v. Mike Love
- Don Felder v. Don Henley and Glenn Frey
- Roger Waters v. David Gilmour
- Ray Davies v. Dave Davies
- Paul Simon v. Art Garfunkel
- Keith Richards v. Elton John
- David Lee Roth v. Eddie Van Halen
- Slash v. Axl Rose
- Oasis v. Blur
- Noel Gallagher v. Liam Gallagher
- Kanye West v. Jay-Z
- NAS v. Jay-Z
- Axl Rose v. Kurt Cobain
- Eminem v. Christina Aguilera
- John Lennon v. Paul McCartney
- Elton John v. Madonna
- Chris Brown v. Drake
- Kid Rock v. Tommy Lee
- 50 Cent v. Ja Rule
- Taylor Swift v. Kanye West
- Mariah Carey v. Jennifer Lopez
- Meek Mill v. Drake
- Lady Gaga v. Madonna
- Tupac v. Biggie.

(Be warned – if you invite Tommy Lee to your dream dinner party, do not play Kid Rock as dinner music!)

another century? Would a tablescape evoking national pride offend a dream dinner party guest from another country?

Tablescapes have evolved. Page through any *Martha Stewart Living* magazine and see that it is possible to replicate entire worlds for the purpose of creating ambience. You are going to yearn for ambience at your dream diner party. The question to ask yourself is how much ambience is too much ambience? And how much ambience is too little ambience? If I am Jesus, and I get resurrected (again) to have dinner someplace, and I show up at the dinner and sit down at a dinner table tablescaped with a vase filled with daffodils and some shamrock confetti strewn about the table and the turkey napkin rings and Santa Claus place cards, I'm going to be all, "Where the fuck am I?" or "I got resurrected (again) for this schizophrenic tablescape?" and will likely walk out. Aristotle sitting down at a table festooned with fake candles or LED lights will likely generate such confusion that anything smart he might have contributed to the dinner party conversation would be extinguished. And how might Napoleon Bonaparte feel sitting down at a table with centerpieces filled with English Roses?

Timing

By definition, the dream dinner party will need to take place at dinner time. Try to negotiate as much time as possible with your guests. You can sleep later. You will only be able to sing with John Lennon and/or paint with Picasso and/or talk silk trading routes with Marco Polo and/or talk inventions with Thomas Edison once.

FOR ALL YOU PHILISTINES...

Most iconic chairs:

- Hans Wegner, *Papa Bear* chair
- Verner Panton, *Stacking Chair*
- Ludwig Mies van der Rohe *Barcelona*
- Warren Platner *Arm Chair*
- Le Corbusier *Grand Confort*
- Thonet *209*
- Eero Saarinen *Tulip*
- Arne Jacobsen *Egg*
- Marcel Breuer *B32/Cesca*
- Eileen Gray *Transat*
- Charles and Ray Eames *Loung and Ottoman* and *LCW*.

IV.   Protocols and Procedures

FAQs

1.   How many guests are permitted?

There are typically three guests at a dream dinner party.

2.   Will guests whose identities are tied into a partner, i.e, Adam and Eve, The Wright Brothers, Lewis and Clark, Bo and Luke Duke, George Michael and Andrew Ridgeley, Darryl Hall and John Oates, count as one guest or two?

You'd think that they would count as one guest. Like, what does John Oates even do? Sadly, though—and typically—eponymous pairs, like Lewis and Clark, count as two guests. This rule is almost always not waivable for it would be possible then to turn a three-person guest list into a six-person guest list if you invited Adam and Eve, Laverne and Shirley, and Batman and Robin to your dream dinner party. The slope gets even slipperier when the connection becomes more ten-

PRO TIP

Whenever Thomas Edison has lobster, he picks it up off his plate and makes it dance while he sings an eerily perfect rendition of B'52's "Rock Lobster," which raises a ton of questions. But be prepared for this, if you invite Thomas Edison to your party and are serving lobster.

CELEBRITY COUPLES WHO COULD THEORETICALLY BE ONE DREAM DINNER PARTY GUEST

- Carly Simon and James Taylor
- Cleopatra and Mark Antony
- Napoleon and Josephine
- Lady Diana and Prince Charles
- Henry VIII and Anne Boleyn
- Queen Victoria and Prince Albert
- Bonnie & Clyde
- Johnny Cash and June Carter
- JFK and Jackie
- Elvis and Priscilla Presley
- Paul and Linda McCartney
- Fred Astaire and Ginger Rogers
- Brooke Shields and Michael Jackson
- Barack and Michelle Obama
- Juan and Eva Peron

- Aphrodite and Adonis
- Orpheus and Eurydice
- Humphrey Bogart and Lauren Bacall
- Diego Rivera and Frida Kahlo
- Mildred and Richard Loving
- Lucy and Desi
- Mork and Mindy
- Mike and Carol Brady
- Kermit and Miss Piggy
- Bert and Ernie
- Jim and Pam
- Sonny and Cher
- Howdy Doody and Buffalo Bob
- Joanie and Chachi
- Luke and Laura
- John Lennon and Yoko Ono
- Grace Kelly and Prince Rainier III
- John and Abigail Adams
- Jay-Z and Beyonce.

uous, when once-coupled duos split and find success individually, like Sonny and Cher or Simon and Garfunkel or Napoleon and Josephine. The slope gets slipperier still when contemplating inviting combative couples so you can witness the fighting, like Alexander Hamilton and Aaron Burr, David and Goliath, Elizabeth Taylor and Richard Burton; or Chris Evert and Martina Navratilova. In such a scenario, where the value of the individual guests is minimal, it's clear the purpose of the invite is to witness a guest's interaction with another guest.

3.   Do people who predeceased guests know those guests' histories?

Generally no. This is very important. If the challenge of explaining Bob Marley to Wolfgang Amadeus Mozart or the challenge of explaining to Thomas Jefferson why he can't have his way with Oprah sounds exhilarating to you then have at it. If, however, such a challenge sounds exhausting and you don't want to spend your limited dream dinner party time making peace with Oprah and Thomas Jefferson when Thomas Jefferson asks her to fetch him some lemonade, then you will want to tailor your dream dinner party guest list appropriately. Though, if your goal, pursuant to Section II, is to cultivate a good skirmish, then mission accomplished. Which brings up another interesting point guests at your dream dinner party typically do not have the option to leave. So pairing longstanding rivals and demanding them to do something—duet or reconcile or hug or fight or otherwise collaborate for your amusement—would be interesting.

An inequity in the stature of dream dinner party guests will foster a hostile dream dinner party environment. And you don't want that. Imagine George Washington dining with two lesser presidents, like Zachary Taylor and Millard Fillmore. Or Karen Carpenter dream dinnering with Celine Dion and Adele.

Could an animal be a guest, i.e. Flipper the Dolphin, Lassie, or a dinosaur?
No. But I guess if you were really into a particular animal then you could inquire about this and request a waiver. I wouldn't suggest it, though, and not just because I'm not really into animals. Animals can't even talk. And they might eat all the food. But if you want Bubbles the Chimp at your dream dinner party, then have at it. Or if you are worried about someone falling down a well, and you want Lassie to let you know when that happens, then by all means, invite Lassie. But then be prepared to have Lassie begging for pot roast.

If, however, you want to extract some dinosaur DNA and seek to do what John Hammond and his team of genetic scientists did on Isla Nublar then it might be worth asking. Like when asked to identify your dream dinner party guests just write down, "T-Rex" and see what happens. You might end up with Barney though.

4.   How much do dream dinner party guests know?

You generally have to bring deceased dinner party guests up to speed. It could be an incredible pain in the ass to spend an entire evening explaining the internet, automobiles, air travel, the moon landing, Michael Jackson, O.J. Simpson, rap music, WW2, Britney Spears, and literally every single thing we tend to talk about at dream dinner parties nowadays to Abraham Lincoln. The last thing we want is for Abraham Lincoln to feel awkward. But if you find the idea of explaining modernity to Abraham Lincoln alluring then have at it.

Let's face it, the learning curve necessary for bringing someone up to speed on the modern state of the world is likely not that steep. We are not as evolved as we think we are. And Abraham Lincoln is surely astonishingly adept at bringing himself up to speed on the current state of the world. Do you want to spend the whole dream dinner party teaching Amelia Earhart about Michael Jackson? No. Is Amelia Earhart more adept than we realize at acquiring knowledge? Yes.

Also, be mindful of what might happen when guests discover that they have schools, roads, airports, cities, and/or holidays named for them. Thomas Jefferson's ego is likely to inflate when he discovers that someone carved his head into a giant mountain and three million people go see it every year. Along with the fat that he has a monument built solely to him near the tidal basin on the National Mall and countless educational institutions, counties, streets, some cities, and at least one Airplane and one Starship named after him,

5.   Can spouses attend?

Spouses can attend, in fact they make great wing people should you wish to extract vital and heretofore unknown and knowable information from a guest, but they will count as a guest.

6. Are there standard penalties imposed for improper dream dinner party behavior?

If at your dream dinner party, you invite someone and murder them—the invitation having been extended for the sole purpose of the murder—will you suffer consequences? No. There are no consequences. The dream dinner party is not to be confused with those other ice-breaking college essay questions about the moral ramifications of going back in history to murder baby Joseph Stalin. There would be no time and history manipulation here. Murdering dream dinner party guest Stalin wouldn't save anyone, and murdering dream dinner party guest Tom Hanks wouldn't spare us from sitting through *Forrest Gump*. It would just be one of those homicides for fun.

EAT ME!

Elvis Pres-leek Soup

This is that thing of when you host a dinner party and make some leek soup, and then you swivel your hips and don't talk to anyone, because a little less conversation.

7. How long will dinner last?

Knowing how much time you will have for both the dinner and, if permitted, the post dinner activities could be a factor in who to invite and what to serve. These dinners are typically at night; typically with a soft deadline of four hours. But if Jesus and Lucille Ball are having a great time then no one is going to make them go home. Make sure you allow yourself enough time if preparing a duet or sporting event.

8. Do I need interpreters/translators? Will they count as one of my guests?

Ancillary to the question of how much guests know. If you invite Otto von Bismarck, Emperor Hirohito, and Haile Selassie to your dream dinner party, will you need to set places for the German, Japanese, and Ethiopian translators? No. Guests come able to speak to one another.

9. Can fictional characters be guests?

Rarely, though I have seen it happen, hosts are permitted to invite fictional characters as dream dinner party guests. This is obviously different from inviting *Raiders of the Lost Ark* Harrison Ford to your dream dinner party. Harrison Ford is real. Dressing him as a fictional character is different than inviting a fictional character to the dream dinner party. Don't assume that when you invite Jason Bourne to your dream dinner party that you're getting Matt Damon as Jason Bourne. Inviting Jason Bourne to your dream dinner party is different than inviting Matt Damon as Jason Bourne. Same with Jo March of *Little Women*, Atticus Finch of *To Kill a Mockingbird*, Vito Corleone of *The Godfather*, or Anton Chigurh in *No Country for Old Men*, a questionable dream dinner party guest to be sure, but you do you.

Again, this is rare, but I have seen it happen. This would not be the quintessential dream dinner party handbook, the only dream dinner party handbook you'll ever need, if my associates and I did not apprise you of this possibility. To that end, some wonderful fictional dream dinner party guests to consider:

a. Childhood Friends
    i. Fern Arable, Pippi Longstocking, Jane Eyre, the Little Prince, Farley Drexel "Fudge" Hatcher, Romeo, Juliet, Tarzan, Nancy Drew, Johnny Cade, Ponyboy, Willy Wonka, Veruca Salt, Dorothy Gale, Ebenezer Scrooge, Robinson Crusoe, Harry Potter, Oliver Twist, Alice

b. Sparring Partners
    i. Tom Ripley, Hamlet, Annie Wilkes, Nurse Ratched, Gandalf, Mark Watney, Lady Macbeth, Gandalf, Lisbeth Salander, Patrick Bateman, Tyler Durden, James Bond, Clarice Starling, the Invisible Man

c. Characters Who Might Need a Hug
    i. Lennie Small, Randle Patrick McMurphy, the Father and/or the Boy from Cormac McCarthy's "The Road", the girl from Shirley Jackson's "The Lottery", Celie, Ophelia, Owen Meany, Celie, Clarissa Dalloway, Sethe, Boo Radley

d. Classic Dudes and Dudettes
    i. Jay Gatsby, Jean Louise "Scout" Finch, Hester Prynne, Bigger Thomas, Ishmael, Moby Dick, Mr. & Mrs. Bridge, Newland Archer, Celie, Huckleberry Finn, Holden Caulfield, Ishmael, Sherlock Holmes, Bigger Thomas, Holly Golightly, Stephen Dedalus, Leopold Bloom, Kurtz, Humbert Humbert, Joe Kavalier, Sam Clay, Dean Moriarty, Dorian Gray, Don Quixote, Santiago, Alex Portnoy, Anna Karenina, Oscar Wao, Adam Trask, Tom Joad, Gregor Samsa

If inclined to include fictional characters as guests at your dream dinner party, you will need to think fast. I've coordinated dream dinner parties where hosts invite three Stephen King villains so they could deduce who was truly the evilest; three favorite children's book characters; three Harry Potter characters; three literary dads (we don't have the pages to unpack that one). Most, though, simply pick three favorites. Once I curated a dream dinner party where the guest chose Meryl Streep in *Out of Africa,* Meryl Streep in *Sophie's Choice,* and Meryl Streep in *The Devil Wears Prada.* When hosts are permitted to pick three fictional guests, hosts typically pick three characters from one favorite book, favorite movie, or favorite TV show.

10.   What if you don't like what you know to be your guest's favorite food or drink?

Let's assume that you are a painter. And you love Cubism. And you love Pablo Picasso. So, you want to invite Pablo Picasso to your dream dinner party. But alas, Pablo's favorite drink is Sangria. And you don't like Sangria. Not only do you not like it, but it gives you hives. Just being in the same room with a glass of Sangria makes you break out into a rash. Can you still invite Pablo Picasso? Yes. This is not a cosmic version of not bringing peanut butter to a cafeteria because your kid goes to school with someone with a peanut allergy. No one gets hives at a dream dinner party.

11.   Will selfies last?

You know that thing of when in movies like *Back to the Future* when the person's existence is called into question due to some cinematic tinkering with the space-time continuum, and then they have to race against time and they look at photographs and the person is starting to fade from the photographs? Like, will that happen? No. If you take a selfie with Vasco de Gama, and you're all into Vasco de Gama and posting him on Instagram and the what-have-you, and then the dream dinner party ends, Vasco de Gama's visage will remain in perpetuity.

12.   Should I invite living people when theoretically, I could just invite them to a regular dinner party?

If you have strong feelings about a currently alive person, then invite them to the dream dinner party. Of course, you could someday win a dinner with Bruce Springsteen or Angela Merkel but the likelihood of that is sufficiently remote to, should you love Springsteen or Merkel, invite them to your dream dinner party.

V.   *The Guide to Frequently Identified Dream Dinner Party Guests*

It'll be important for you to develop a general mission statement in advance of selecting your dream dinner party guests. What is the mission here? Is it to break bread with people you admire? Be careful. What will knowing that the Buddha has a flatulence problem or that Jesus tends to chew with his mouth open do to your faith? Or is the mission of your dream dinner party to learn? Or to grow as a person?

Perhaps your mission statement will be more benign. Like, you just might really want to hear what a collaboration between John Lennon, Jimi Hendrix, and Jim Morrison might sound like. And that three to four minutes of ecstasy, or at least the quenching of your curiosity, is all that you ask. Pizza and chicken wings are fine after that. Or maybe you want to know what a duet between Abraham Lincoln and Karen Carpenter might sound like. That would be interesting. But then again, as the host, do you have the absolute authority to command your guests to sing? What if Abraham Lincoln—or John Lennon or Jim Morrison, for that matter—doesn't want to sing?

Inherent in any selection is the knowledge that someone you hold in high regard might turn out to be a jerk. Like that time I got lost at Disney World and wandered into the employee break area and saw Mickey Mouse smoking a Pall Mall. Are you ready for this? Are you prepared for all the pre-#MeToo era men to expect the women to serve them at your dream dinner party? Or, what if Mark Twain asks Katherine Graham to light his pipe? You will be spending your entire dream dinner brokering peace. Not fun.

If your intent is self-advancement, then perhaps inviting the head of Goldman Sachs is the way to go. "Here are some appetizers. And my resume." Or a paragon of whatever industry in which you seek advancement? "Welcome Ralph Lauren. I'm wearing an original design." You might want some reassurance, however, that these guests are there willingly and that whomever granted you the dream dinner party has not kidnapped your living guests.

And decide if you even *want* to waste a spot on a living guest. Sure, Meryl Streep or Steven Spielberg or Bill Gates or Mark Zuckerberg or Oprah Winfrey will have immediate benefits. But you could, metaphysically speaking, dine with them anytime.

The Top Ten

These are the top ten vote-getters in our dream dinner party guest poll.

1. Abraham Lincoln

Lincoln was the leading vote getter in our poll. Furthermore, those who identified Abraham Lincoln as one of their dream dinner party guests generally identified him first, just as reflexively as though a doctor were hitting your knee with one of those reflex hammers. Let me be the first one to say this and please repeat aloud after me, "It's ok" ["it's ok"] "to not invite" ["to not invite"] "Abraham Lincoln" ["Abraham Lincoln"] "to my dream dinner party." ["to my dream dinner party."] Very good. See how easy that was? The Civil War has a sort of gravitational pull to it. Like, there are Civil War reenactors who, by their very definition, reenact the Civil War. Like, have you ever heard of a War of 1812 reenactor? Me neither. Why is the Civil War the only conflict that gets reenacted?

There are several ancillary benefits to inviting Lincoln to your dream dinner party, however. Ask him to read The Gettysburg Address as your voicemail greeting; probe him for insight into the general governance strategies; probe him for scoop on other historical figures like did Ulysses Grant have bad breath and how did it *feel* when you toured Gettysburg and whose idea was it to go to the play that night and was it really not that good as the heralded joke suggests?

Getting him up to speed on the state of our union, the state of our culture, the state of everything, would be a huge pain in the ass, expend the majority of the time allotted for your dream dinner party, and inevitably result in making Abraham Lincoln very, very sad. Granted, you could be the one to explain to Lincoln that as a direct result of his leadership, the Union survived and then women could vote and then we beat Nazis and then there was a black Supreme Court justice and then we put a man on the moon and then America elected a black man president and then right after that a two-bit muskrat-headed television con man fuckbonnet was elected president. Also, you always run the risk of gaping-head-wound-Lincoln showing up at your dream dinner party; no "wow" factor here—"who'd you have at your dream dinner party?" "Lincoln." "Oh cool. Want to go to the mall later?" He's, like, so basic.

Pairs well with: other world leaders; if skirmishes are your thing, then Jefferson Davis and Robert E. Lee might be fun; any deceased relative who is super into the Civil War, i.e. every dad and grandpa who has ever lived; readers of George Saunders' *Lincoln in the Bardo* might be tempted to invite Lincoln's dead son to the dream dinner party just to observe that reunion; to finally determine whether Lincoln was gay, you could invite Judy Garland to the dream dinner party and see if he's, like, super into her; you could also invite the cast of *Magic Mike* and ask them to perform and see if Lincoln is into them too. That would be both an entertaining dream dinner party and a historically relevant one. Daniel Day-Lewis won an Oscar in 2011 for playing Abraham Lincoln in Steven Spielberg's *Lincoln*. If you are super into Lincoln, you could invite both Abraham Lincoln and Daniel Day-Lewis in his Lincoln costume and have a Lincoln-off.

2. William Shakespeare

William Shakespeare was the second leading vote-getter in our poll. I'm not sure why. Again, it almost felt like some sort of knee-jerk reaction. Like, this is who I am *supposed* to be inviting to my dream dinner party. But take a deep breath. If you didn't like him in high school and/or college, then why would you want him at your dream dinner party? I did not like him in college, and I would not like him talking all fancy at my dream dinner party.

If you are determined to dine with Shakespeare, you would be advised to request "the man who wrote the plays currently credited to a man named William Shakespeare." There are many weaknesses in the case for Shakespeare, most significantly how a dramatist of his era would have such intimate knowledge of aristocracy and royalty. I am of the school of thought that Edward de Vere, the Earl of Oxford, wrote Shakespeare's plays, or at least co-authored them with William Shakespeare. The works of Shakespeare, however, are clearly the works of an aristocrat, which Shakespeare was not.

Benefits are many. You can talk to him about his writing process and if he knew that his plays would still resonate hundreds of years later, i.e., if he knew that he would be *Shakespeare*; ask him directly if he wrote all the plays and maybe ask him to prove it; maybe ask him to write a new play if he has enough time—imagine the money you could get from a brand-new Shakespeare play. You could also just find out what he looked like.

However, potential negatives are many also. I bet knowing that people now considered him the greatest writer of all time would give him license to talk about himself the whole time. And it would rhyme. And be in iambic pentameter. And all the guests would just be, like, "what the fuck is with this guy?" Or you invite the guy known as Shakespeare, and he turns out to be the complete phony that people suspect he is, and you have just wasted a dream dinner party spot.

Pairs well with: Other writers of his era; other writers generally.

3. Barack Obama

Our third highest vote-getter. Well ahead of … you know who. Respondents cited his poise and relaxed candor as being an asset to any dinner party. He would put anyone at ease. Some guests also thought it would be a hoot to share a cigarette with him. Just something to say they did. Like going skydiving or walking on the moon or hitting a home run in Game 7 of the World Series.

For a lesson in grace and dignity and patience, there could be no better guest. Though, can these things be taught? Bask in his wisdom and awesomeness. Smoke cigarettes with him. Play basketball with him. Or chess. Or checkers. Or backgammon. You will be a better person for having spent an evening in his midst. Invite Beyonce and Michelle and reenact that inaugural dance from January 20, 2009. And revel. Were you feeling exploitative, you could secretly film him saying something incendiary, like, "Go fuck yourself, Donald." Or, if you wanted to waste a guest spot, why not invite Donald to dinner and not serve well-done steak with ketchup and invite the men to debate. About anything. Obama could make him cry.

PRO TIP

Gandhi fancies himself a connoisseur about *everything*. He once told a host (I won't name names) when referring to the host's chicken tikka masala, that he was a "little bit over enthusiastic with the turmeric" and it's just like "really Gandhi?"

Obviously, there are no cons. Invite this man to your dream dinner party. If there was a con, it would be the fact that he is still alive and so technically you wouldn't need to use a dream dinner party guest spot on him since you might be able to have dinner with him someday somehow some way. Like, whenever he has dinner, the person with whom he is having dinner is basically living your dream dinner party. Which hardly seems just.

Pairs well with: Hillary Rodham Clinton for a frank, immersive discussion about 2008; Joe Biden for a study in friendship; MLK, Frederick Douglass, Harriet Tubman, Muhammad Ali, James Baldwin, W.E.B. DuBois, Malcolm X, Thurgood Marshall for a frank and immersive discussion on progress; Michael Jordan, Larry Bird, LeBron James, Kobe Bryant, or Phil Jackson to discuss or play basketball; if you're super into Agriculture then his Secretary of Agriculture Tom Vilsack; or any other member of his cabinet corresponding to what you're into, like if you're super into commerce then invite former Secretary of Commerce Penny Pritzker.

And if you really want your dream dinner party to be controversial, ask President Obama to wear his tan suit.

4. Martin Luther King, Jr.

Those who put him at the top of our very scientific poll cited their eagerness to just shake hands with him as sufficient reason for so doing. They quite simply want to pay homage to this man. This is noble. And authentic. He would add an element of grace and authority to any evening. And imagine having MLK, Obama, and Malcolm X all at dinner together. What we like about MLK as an invitee is that there can be no ulterior motive for the invite. Unlike Van Gogh or John Lennon, who "might be willing" to leave you with a new and priceless creation, dining with MLK would be simply for the experience.

Some lessons on pacifism, maintaining serenity and composure, turning the other cheek, and protesting nonviolently wouldn't do anyone any harm. Imagine being able to smile while being berated by your boss?

Pairing MLK with Donald…you know that would be fun. How awesome would it be to watch MLK beat the shit out of him? You could videotape and sell that. So, there are some financial benefits to inviting MLK to your dream dinner party.

Pairs well with: Mahatma Gandhi—who served as a model for MLK's pacifism and the civil rights movement in general—and MLK dinner party would be something. Barack Obama, Rosa Parks, Frederick Douglass, Harriet Tubman, Muhammad Ali, James Baldwin, Mary McLeod Bethune, Shirley Chisholm, W.E.B. DuBois, Michael Jordan, Malcolm X, Thurgood Marshall, Jackie Robinson, Sojourner Truth, August Wilson, Booker T. Washington.

5. Mahatma Gandhi

I understand this one, to be in this man's presence would likely infuse one's life with a new and unparalleled serenity, humility, compassion, and contentment. But you should also know that Gandhi had no teeth, kept a set of false teeth in his loin cloth, and inserted them only when he ate. If you can stomach this— not to mention the loin cloth—and still have a yearning for some inspiration, then you really can do no better than Gandhi.

This one, while we are being frank about people's true colors, could be problematic insofar as his bizarre and abusive treatment of his grandnieces belies an extreme attitude towards women, despite what he said publicly regarding equality. If your devotion to or respect for Gandhi because of his commitment to nonviolent resistance, and/or ethnic amity supersedes your repulsion to his sexual proclivities then that's fine. But prepare your guests.

Diet was an integral part of Gandhi's philosophy. He frequently fasted and eschewed alcohol. Make sure if he is one of your dream dinner party guests, he is not in one of his fasting periods. Or that you serve something antithetical to his mission or philosophy.

Gandhi pairs well with other revolutionaries, both violent and nonviolent. A conversation between yourself, Gandhi, MLK, and Jesus would be interesting, if you're into that sort of thing. A conversation between yourself, Gandhi, Oliver Cromwell, and George Washington would be a bit more animated. Also consider other revolutionaries, both pacifist and violent, and architects of revolutions: William Wallace, Simon Bolivar, Che Guevara, Vladimir Lenin, Fidel Castro, Susan B. Anthony, and Voltaire. You could also invite Ben Kingsley, who won an Oscar in 1983 for his portrayal of Gandhi in Richard Attenborough's *Gandhi*, and Ben and Gandhi could have a Gandhi-off. You could live-tweet the Gandhi-off.

BREAKING THE ICE

John Lennon

DO ask: What's your favorite Beatles song?

DON'T ask: What's the deal with Yoko?

6. Jesus Christ

I wonder how Jesus feels being sixth in our poll. Like, he made the top ten, and he's behind some heavy hitters—MLK, Lincoln, BARACK!!!—but the fact he's behind anyone could really piss him off.

There's a host of reasons to invite this guy to your dream dinner party. Number one reason of which I can think is to invite him along with an evangelical of your choice—either a big one, like Pat Robertson or Jerry Falwell or Franklin Graham or that weasel faced Joel Osteen, or even a minor one, like your crazy uncle—and sit there while Jesus berates the evangelical for the inherent hypocrisy in everything he or she does and says. That would be awesome. Though, you'd waste a dream dinner party spot on an evangelical. Totally up to you.

Before committing to anything, however, you will need to determine what, if any, restrictions there are on Jesus. Would he be allowed to do miracles? If so, how many and what kind of miracles? Like "raising Lazarus from the dead" caliber miracles or "turning water into wine" sort of miracles, should you run out of wine (which should never ever happen at any dinner party but especially a dream dinner party)? Like, could you bring people back from the dead? Like loved ones and pets? Even if not, could you film the ordinary miracles he did do? Although, a miracle on film would be subject to doubters, given the proliferation of CGI and other image manipulation available to regular consumers. You could also ask Jesus for answers to all the world's greatest mysteries: Who killed JFK? Where is Jimmy Hoffa? What is the deal with Stonehenge? The Loch Ness monster? Bigfoot? The lost city of Atlantis? The lost Roanoke colony? What happened on the Mary Celeste? Who wrote Shakespeare's plays? Ted Cruz is the Zodiac killer, isn't he? What's in Area 51? Where is Amelia Earhart? And you could also ask him for answers to your own personal questions too. What is the secret ingredient in Aunt Connie's cole slaw? How does Aunt Myrna get her fried chicken so crispy? Was Uncle Jeb the original Night Stalker? Though, I suspect that even Jesus would have limits. And your other guests would presumably want to ask him questions too. Though to preserve your questions, you could invite JFK to be a dream dinner party guest and then JFK would ask Jesus, "Who killed me?"

There are also a host of reasons not to invite this guy to your dream dinner party. There could be no gluttony. Or sloth. Or pride. Like, you couldn't say, "I am so proud of this souffle" because Jesus would get mad. There could be no cursing. There could be no gossip. There could be no berating people.

Lastly, if you saw Jesus do a miracle, would what you have still be considered faith if you no longer require any faith? Isn't faith the belief of something for which there is no proof? If you have proof of something, what happens to the faith that existed before the proof?

Pairs well with other religious founders. Like, how about Jesus, Muhammad, and Siddhartha Gautama all get together and argue why their religion is the best?

7. John Lennon

This is risky. It seems to me that all this guy would do is talk about himself. Or engage in some sort of protest. Or sing everything. And you'd have to play the Beatles all night or be criticized for not playing more from the Plastic Ono Band catalog or subject yourself to incessant criticism of anything else you might choose to play. And in light of the fact that his two sons and wife Yoko are still alive, you run the risk that he would spend his time trying to phone them. Or text them, once you explained to him what texting was. That said, how awesome would it be to have John Lennon lead a dream dinner party sing-along, if you're into that sort of thing?

But for those who are into the Beatles, and I believe there are many, the benefits of sitting down with one of its founders might outweigh the risk that he is non-responsive or evasive or preoccupied with thoughts of Yoko. Imagine hearing firsthand how he founded the Beatles, what his childhood was like, the circumstances, ideas, nuances and rationales behind a song. Or what it felt like that night, February 9, 1964, when the Beatles performed on the Ed Sullivan show. Imagine getting his real thoughts about Paul, peace, Penny Lane, and the present state of music.

He would pair well with the other Beatles. If you want to get very, very, very rich from the dream dinner party, invite the Beatles to sing a song together, record that song, and then sell that song. I think, though, that in inviting other Beatles, you run the risk of creating some sort of skirmish stemming from old rivalries.

He would pair well with almost anyone in music: Karen Carpenter, Aretha Franklin, Elvis Presley, Freddie Mercury, Bob Marley (imagine a Lennon / Marley duet?), Johnny Cash, David Bowie, Whitney Houston, Janis Joplin, Prince. You just have to sort of insert your own favorite.

I've always wondered what a John Lennon and Steve Perry from Journey duet might sound like. They both have this pure tone that is intriguing. Same with Michael Stipe. But do you want to waste dream dinner party invites on Steve Perry and/or Michael Stipe? Especially now, when sound engineers can just do a Nat King Cole / Natalie Cole "Unforgettable" thing.

Also, putting John Lennon and Jesus Christ together at a dinner is always fun. They both engage in a flex fest given they both think they're rulers of the universe.

8. John F. Kennedy

Respondents who included JFK as one of their top dream dinner party guests cited the fact that he would provide valuable sophistication and refinement. Recall the pictures of him in a top hat at his inauguration; or in loafers and wayfarers on sailboats; or with him and Jacqueline strolling through George-town or relaxing in Hyannis Port; or any number of pictures of him smoking a cigar.

For fans of the Kennedys, and I believe there are several, this dream dinner party guest would provide much needed answers to several lingering mysteries and valuable insight to several intriguing events from and around his presiden-cy. There are so many secrets to unearth here. I am as big a fan of the Kenne-dys as they come, and part of the allure is the mystique. To *know* the answers to the questions surrounding the family and the family dynamics or to hear JFK say something negative or disparaging about someone (I don't know what I would do if he said something negative about Jacqueline) or to learn that he had horrible body odor or that he chewed loudly or to see him stare at another guest lasciviously would be devastating (and you do not want to know the over-under on this last possibility). Inevita-bly, questions regarding extra marital activities would arise, and

PRO TIP

JFK's favorite dessert is, not surprisingly, Boston Cream Pie. What is surprising is that his favorite beer is Heineken. In fact, he refuses to drink Sam Adams, calling it "too hoppy."

do you really want to spend your dream dinner party talking about adultery? It might make some guests feel very uncomfortable. (*See,* Jesus.)

There are those reading this awesome, scientifically researched book who have more nefarious intentions. For them, a dream dinner party of John Kennedy, Robert Kennedy, and Marilyn Monroe would be fun. I can't condone this, but I owe it to my readers to identify plausible dream dinner party guest combinations for all audiences. What about John Kennedy, Nikita Khrushchev, and Fidel Castro eating dinner together?

You will likewise recall that John Kennedy had two brothers who also died tragically while serving their country. Robert F. Kennedy was assassinated in Los Angeles in June 1968 after winning the California democratic primary. Joseph Kennedy, Jr. was killed in August 1944 while serving as a bomber pilot when a plane full of explosives in which he was riding blew up. A reunion of these three could be really cool. If you are into that sort of thing. And, while not a new Van Gogh painting, it could

PRO TIP

Billboard 100's number one song the day Princess Diana died was "Mo' Money Mo' Problems" by Notorious BIG featuring Puff Daddy and MASE. As such, she will insist on listening to it throughout dinner, so have it at the ready or she'll pout. Also, she does this weird dance when it plays.

be of some value. An ancillary benefit of inviting Joseph P. Kennedy, Jr. to your dream dinner party is being able to interview him for the very first time, about what, if any, political aspirations he had. By all accounts, he was smarter and more effervescent and personable and politically inclined than his brother John. To verify this would be both interesting and historically relevant. To see JFK and his son, John F Kennedy, Jr., toss the football around on the beach in Hyannis Port, MA would be life altering.

9. Paul Rudd / Mother Teresa (tie)

Tied for 9th place are Paul Rudd and Mother Teresa.

As of this writing, Paul Rudd is being lauded for beginning a text thread with a 7th grader who had no classmates sign his yearbook. He did this without fan fare or any expectation of anything in return. Additionally, he can do action as Ant Man in the Marvel Universe, he can do comedy as the bumbling best friend, and he can do romance as the husband about to turn 40.

He is always fun, always up to party, always doing nice things for people without expectation of anything in return, and just always kind.

Pairs well with: any comedian, any child in need of a self-esteem boost, any one.

Mother Teresa on the other hand, is always scowling, never fun, looks like an old potato, and is always walking around in front of television cameras pretending to help people. I am so tired of this bitch. Why are people still so into her? She is a horrible idea for a host of reasons. But first, let's get to the flawed thinking that prompts people to pick Mother Teresa as a dream dinner party guest. Do they think, like Jesus Christ (see above) her unparalleled altruism will rub off on them? Do they really find her that interesting? What's so interesting about her? It would seem to me that all Mother would do is scowl and pout at the gluttony of the whole affair. What sort of contribution is that to your dream dinner party? But no matter, any appetite you might have had would be squelched by looking at her squinched-up potato face. No thanks.

Also, who names someone "Mother"? The whole dinner would suddenly adopt a profoundly Pencey hue. "Please pass the mashed potatoes, Mother."

Pairs well with: No one. Except maybe that other over-exalted asshole, Tom Hanks.

Goodbye Mother. Or Teresa. Or whatever the fuck your name is.

10. Princess Diana

One of the wealthy people Mother Teresa excepted from her universal disdain for the wealthy, inclusion of this one, like John F. Kennedy, in our scientific poll of most oft-requested dream dinner party guests is simultaneously wholly expected and sort of superfluous.

Princess Diana would add an aura of sophistication and refinement to any dream dinner party. For Princess Diana aficionados—and Princess Diana had (has) the sort of aura which cultivates aficionados—just being in her midst is sufficient reason to include her as a dream dinner party guest. Taking pictures with and of Princess Diana, provided the host or hostess can take and keep photos, might be sufficient reason alone.

There are some potential substantive benefits here. I think there would be so much to unearth here with respect to her story, her psyche, her disappointments, and the whole fairytale thing.

You run the risk, however, of her spending all her time and attention Googling Harry and Will and Kate and Meghan and her grandchildren. You couldn't really fault her for that. If you can get some sort of guarantee that after a cursory update on Will and Kate and Harry and Meghan, Princess Diana will give you her full and undivided attention and speak with vulnerability and authenticity about her life as a young bride and young mother and then tabloid target, then this is a solid selection. I mean, she's already dead, so speaking honestly and openly shouldn't really be too big of an ask for her.

Pairs well with: Jacqueline Bouvier Kennedy Onassis, Princess Grace, Audrey Hepburn, other princessy type people. Those who are into princesses would revel in the tsunami of refinement that such pairings would create.

The Artists / The Creators

The people who create have a monopoly on the top spots of our dream dinner party survey. Rightly or wrongly, we revere these people. Unlike kings and queens and presidents, our reverence is voluntary. We identify with the characters they portrayed and the words they wrote. There is probably some flaw in the human central nervous system which makes us unable to compartmentalize and segregate emotions very well or that our perception of reality is askew.

But it's so fun.

Movies

Long-deceased movie stars and directors are ranked surprisingly high in our scientific poll of dream dinner party invitees. I say surprisingly because there are just as many potential negatives attached to each as potential benefits. Among the potential negatives are: Since every single movie star of yester year smoked cigarettes, it is likely that upon being resurrected to attend your dinner, they will expect to smoke cigarettes throughout the dream dinner party. It would be awful if, adhering to the social mores of their day, they lit up a Chesterfield only to be met with scorn and derision from other guests and spend the rest of the dream dinner party sulking.

PRO TIP

Any kind of cheese can cause Alfred Hitchcock to become severely flatulent. It is best to avoid cheese—or dairy of any kind—when Hitchcock is eating.

Frances McDormand – If the three roles for which she has won Oscars – *Fargo, Three Billboards Outside Ebbing, Missouri,* and *Nomadland,* are any indication, McDormand would be a highly versatile and therefore, highly valuable guest. Versatility is important in these situations. She will have no idea what she is walking into. Furthermore, inviting her with other actors who have won three or more Oscars could be highly fun. Imagine an act off between Frances, Meryl, and Katherine Hepburn? Or Frances, Jack Nicholson, and Daniel Day Lewis? Or invite Frances, Meryl, and Tom Hanks (who has but two Oscars (and a son named Chet)) and make Tom Hanks sit in the corner.

Remember, all these potential dream dinner party guests are real people with real feelings.

Denzel Washington – This is a popular choice with the ladies. Verify that fornication is possible if that is the goal of inviting him to your dream dinner party.

Buster Keaton and/or Charlie Chaplin – If you are a fan of this era of film, or film in general, then these two are logical choices. Both would surely have stories about that era of film.

Audrey Hepburn – This could be interesting. She seems like a nice lady. But what if she has a flatulence issue? What if she's really not that nice? At the very least, she would add some refinement to your dream dinner party. Though it might be important to determine before making your selections which guest—and which Audrey Hepburn—you're getting. If you're getting *Breakfast at Tiffany's* Audrey, then hooray. But if you're getting humanitarian Audrey, then that might be a buzzkill.

PRO TIP

Audrey Hepburn drinks gravy. If you must have gravy at your dream dinner party, don't invite Audrey Hepburn. If you must have Audrey Hepburn at your dream dinner party, don't serve gravy. Trust me.

James Dean – This could be very cool. Showing him that he still epitomizes cool and is otherwise coolness incarnate would be an honor. Who wouldn't love to hear that they—decades after their death—epitomize cool?

Alfred Hitchcock – I don't like to gossip, but I heard that Hitchcock could get a little "handsy" on set. You don't want him getting "handsy" at your dream dinner party. That said, though, you run the risk of a guest getting "handsy" for anyone whose entire lives happened before the mores of today became mores. Movie buffs would love to talk moviemaking with him. Those who he entertained and terrified might just like to say thanks.

Grace Kelly – I like this selection. Imagine a dinner party with Grace Kelly, Jacqueline Bouvier Kennedy Onassis, and Princess Diana (see above) at a dinner. Or Meghan Markle. Or Rita Hayworth. Or Wallis Simpson. That would be very cool. Hopefully, post-death, these women would be more forthright and revealing than they were when they were alive. Did you ever regret leaving Hollywood to become the princess of Monaco? Did you really deserve the 1954 Best Actress Oscar for your role as Georgie Elgin in *The Country Girl* or should Judy Garland have won for her role as Vicki Lester in *A Star is Born*? You do run the risk of Grace Kelly being saddened by the fate of her children and therefore not being that much fun at dinner. If you could be assured that she wouldn't be trying to call Prince Andrew or Princess Stephanie every five minutes, and if you are into princesses, then I can recommend this selection.

Woody Allen – There was a time when this would have been a sound pick, both because he is surely very interesting and a good conversationalist, but also because if he liked you he could put you in one of his movies. But now – post-Soon-Yi and post-pedophilia-charges – it's just a bad idea. I also bet his self-loathing, insecure, hypochondriacal schtick gets old after a while too.

Tom Hanks – No way. Just don't do it. Ever see an interview with Tom Hanks? All he does is talk about himself. And he does this fake acting thing – like he's the greatest thespian who has ever lived in the whole world. I don't want this to be all gossipy, but Tom Hanks once showed up at a party out of nowhere, quickly found his way into the host's bedroom. He laid down on her bed and started playing with her cat. He stayed on the bed with the cat for over half of the party. The whole time he was texting pictures of him and the cat to his wife Rita Wilson. I know this because he told the host who told me. Then he started talking to this other guy about their signs, and he dropped lots of weird "facts" about Cancers like, "I'm a Cancer, so I can't be around loud noises." And, "I can't use a blow-dryer because I'm a Cancer." Just bizarre. I guess he wasn't really *the worst*, but everyone was ready for him to leave.

Katherine Hepburn – I think of all the old movie stars, she would be one of the most fun. And able to provide lots of insight regarding her costars. The problem, though, is that she wrote a best-selling autobiography in the early 1990s called *Me* in addition to a memoir about the making of *The African Queen*. It's like, "we get it Kathy." How much more insight could she possibly provide?

Spike Lee – He is always interesting and always fine with pizza, so long as it doesn't come from Sal's Famous. There was this one time though that he was at a dinner with Charlie Chaplin who refused to speak and mimed everything. Spike could only take so much. So inviting him with Charlie Chaplin could result in fisticuffs if Chaplin refuses to talk again.

Jimmy Stewart – This is a tough one. To have George *Fucking* Bailey at your dream dinner party would be a rather sizable get. But what if he's a jerk? Or chews with his mouth open? Or what if by selecting him, you get ninety-something year old Jimmy Stewart and you have to puree his dinner for him?
Gary Cooper – In a way, I have this guy to thank for my name. The apex of the popularity of the name "Gary" was 1954, several decades prior to my birth. That was the same year Gary Cooper won his Best Actor Academy Award for his role in High Noon, when 37,898 Garys were born. Like any other actor or actress, there are those who surely revere him.

John Wayne – Folks of a certain generation love this guy, machismo and toughness incarnate. Would not pair well with anyone with any ethnicity.

Meryl Streep – I understand this one. But unless you are an aspiring actor and want an evening's worth of acting tips from Meryl Streep, I just wouldn't expend an invite on her. She's alive. You could conceivably end up sitting next to her on an airplane. On a six-hour flight. Though, of course, she wouldn't be obligated to talk to you. Invite her to your dream dinner party and you could recreate some of Meryl's most classic scenes: like when Robert Redford shampoos her tresses and then pours water over her head in *Out of Africa*, except you could be Robert Redford; or you could install a radiation detector at your house and make her walk through it like she did in *Silkwood;* or invite her to jump on the bed with you like she does in *Mamma Mia!;* or do that thing of when she has to choose between her two kids in *Sophie's Choice*. You could ask her to choose between your two kids. A big benefit, unless you

invite Meryl and Jesus together, is you could get gossip on all the movie stars with whom Meryl has worked. Though, she is likely too refined and classy to reveal too much. You could also invite her and the real Karen Silkwood and after dinner have a Silkwood-off! And the lady who is the most Silkwoody gets a prize!! Also, inviting three different Meryl Streep characters could be fun.

Cher – Speaking of Silkwood, another good person to invite with Abraham Lincoln to determine if he is gay or not. Invite her to sing her hit 1999 song "Believe", and if he's into it then he is likely gay.

Steven Spielberg – Someone super into film would love some one-on-one time with Steven Spielberg. If this is you, then why not invite Spielberg, Hitchcock, and Kubrick to your dream dinner party. Though it seems like you could learn more from just watching and re-watching their films.

Martin Scorsese – I think if you are super into a particular film of his, like if you did a senior thesis on *Taxi Driver* or *GoodFellas* or something, then by all means invite him to your dream dinner party to test your thesis or just chat over some Italian cuisine.

Francis Ford Coppola – It seems like there are enough biographies and interviews and analyses of this guy so that you wouldn't need to use a spot in your dream dinner party to get to know him. But if that's your deal, then go for it. Martin Scorsese and Francis Ford Coppola would fight the entire time over who knows the mob better. Maybe pair the two of them with Al Capone and then they can really hang out with a member of the mob.

Orson Welles – This guy has emerged as one of the most intriguing figures of the 20th century. I imagine an appeal to inviting him to your dream dinner party would be to get some resolution to this whole Rosebud thing from *Citizen Kane*. But isn't some of the fun of mysteries the fact that they are mysteries? Imagine if you gave Orson Welles one of your allotted dream dinner party spots just to get a complete understanding of Rosebud and he arrived and when asked, said "It's the sled. Now pass the mashed potatoes." That would be disappointing, wouldn't it?

Cary Grant – This guy would add a touch of refinement to any dream dinner party.

Sidney Poitier – Obviously the star of *Guess Who's Coming to Dinner* belongs at any dinner so you can say, "Guess who's coming to dinner?" You can also say, "Would you like more mashed potatoes Sidney Poitier?" which is always fun.

FOR ALL YOU PHILISTINES...

Famous recluses:
- J.D. Salinger
- Howard Hughes
- Great Garbo
- Harper Lee
- Emily Dickinson
- Syd Barrett
- Bill Watterson
- Thomas Pynchon
- Dave Chappelle
- Marcel Proust
- Ingvar Kamprad
- Bobby Fischer
- Theodore Kaczynski
- Stanley Kubrick
- Lauryn Hill
- Cormac McCarthy
- Edvard Munch
- Axl Rose
- Yves Saint Laurent
- Brian Wilson
- Batman
- Kenneth Dart
- Nikola Tesla.

Literature

Our research indicates that extending dream dinner party invitations to authors is not just for bibliophiles. Anyone interested in discussing the issues with which a writer grappled in his or her day and how those issues resonate today would be wise to invite an author. Plus, it makes the dream dinner party host seem smart.

Inviting an author as a dream dinner party guest also provides an opportunity for a long-deceased author to write something new. Which might not seem like a big deal except in the literary world (of which authors of Dream Dinner

Party Handbooks are surely a part).

Ernest Hemingway – People love this guy. I get it. Just so we are clear, the "For Sale: baby shoes. Never worn." short story is often attributed to him, but such attribution is unsubstantiated and similar stories predate him. So, inviting him and asking him to give you "another baby shoes six word" story might be met with confusion. If you are a man's man, and like cigars and hunting things with bazookas and going fishing, then having Hemingway at your dream dinner party makes sense.

Alex Haley – The man who raised awareness about the true nature of black history and prompted millions to think about the lives of slaves and blacks' complex genealogy is always a fascinating guest.

Anne Rice – Those into vampires and mistresses of the night and all that stuff are advised to invite her to your dream dinner party. She would pair well with pagans, occultists, Satanists, or really anyone who dabbles in the dark arts.

J.D. Salinger – This could be a huge get. Salinger, a recluse for most of his life following the 1951 publication of *The Catcher in the Rye* until his death in 2010, wrote what many consider one of the best English-language novels of the 20th century and very little, just a few short stories, after that. Inviting him to your dream dinner party would likely make him uncomfortable, and that somehow seems wrong, as does inviting him to your dream dinner party just to ogle him or take a bunch of pictures of him. Though, perhaps in the afterlife he is less reclusive. If you are a recluse, then a dream dinner party filled with other recluses could be a lot of fun for you.

F. Scott Fitzgerald – Everyone has read *The Great Gatsby*. He inspired a generation of writers, despite the fact he died at age 44. His fifth novel, *The Last Tycoon,* was unfinished when he died.

Louisa May Alcott – If *Little Women* is your favorite book, and if you identify with or model your life after one of the March sisters, then inviting Louisa May Alcott to your dream dinner party would make sense. Otherwise, I can't see how she would be much fun.

Ottessa Moshfegh – Her novel *Eileen* is one of the best I have ever read. So was *My Year of Rest and Relaxation*. Conversation would be lively and unconventional and challenging. The titular Eileen ruminates and fantasizes about impaling herself with an icicle, "Perhaps it would have soared down my throat, scraping the vacuous center of my body—I liked to picture these things—and followed through to my guts, finally parting my nether regions like a glass dagger."

Emily Dickinson – I'm into this. Did you know that only ten of Emily Dickinson's poems were published in her lifetime? How fun to invite her to your dream dinner party so she can see her elevation into the canon of great poets. Louisa May Alcott, Emily Dickinson and Jane Austen would probably have lots to discuss about trying to succeed as a writer in a male dominated industry, especially at their time periods.

Edgar Allen Poe – If your dream dinner party is in October, and you are really into tales of mystery and the macabre, then inviting Edgar Allen Poe to your dream dinner party to read *The Raven* makes sense.

Maya Angelou – Imagine Maya Angelou reading "Still I Rise" or "On the Pulse of Morning" at the outset of your dream dinner party.

Robert Frost – Imagine Robert Frost reading "The Gift Outright" or "Stopping By Woods on Snowy Evening" at the outset of your dream dinner party. You could invite Frost, JFK, and Chief Justice Earl Warren and do a John Kennedy Inauguration reenactment. That would be fun.

Toni Morrison – If you need inspiration.

Langston Hughes – If you want to be challenged and inspired.

Jack Kerouac – One of the founders of the literary movement known as the Beat Generation, the message of Kerouac, who died young, reverberates today as millennials, soured by the greed and work habits of the boomers, eschew economic materialism, question standard tenets of authority, and seek spiritual enlightenment. He could be

FAVORITE FOODS OF AUTHORS YOU MAY WISH TO INVITE:

- George Orwell: Plum pudding
- Agatha Christie: Devonshire cream
- Jack Kerouac: Apple pie
- J.D. Salinger: Roast beef
- Jean-Paul Sartre: Halva
- Truman Capote: Italian summer pudding
- Walt Whitman: Coffee cake
- Sylvia Plath: Tomato soup cake
- Willa Cather: Kolaches
- John Steinbeck: Posole
- F. Scott Fitzgerald: Turkey leftovers
- Franz Kafka: Milk
- Edgar Allen Poe: Eggnog
- Ray Bradbury: Pizza soup
- Ernest Hemingway: Hamburgers
- Allen Ginsberg: Cold vegetarian borscht
- Pearl S. Buck: Sweet and sour fish
- Friedrich Nietzsche: Lemon risotto
- Harper Lee: Crackling bread
- Emily Dickinson: Gingerbread
- Edna St. Vincent Millay: Blueberry pie
- Leo Tolstoy: Macaroni and cheese
- Alice B. Toklas: Mushroom sandwiches

having a moment, and wouldn't that be something if you get in on it early by inviting him to your dream dinner party? Also, he would love to see the Britney Spears' movie *Crossroads*, which is basically the *On the Road* of the new millennium.

Stephen King – This guy would definitely be interesting. And imagine the scary story he could tell after or during dessert? But he also seems like the type of guy who would be ok saying, "I don't feel like telling a story now," and so what if he doesn't feel like telling a story after dessert? Why is he even there?

Franz Kafka – If you are into this guy then have at it. I can't recommend this, though. He'd probably be weird, like "eat mashed potatoes with his hands" sort of weird. Though, it would be nice to tell Franz Kafka that the term "Kafkaesque" has become a word which means that something has a nightmarishly complex, bizarre, or illogical quality. He might either be very upset or very proud of this. Probably proud, though. Getting your name to be a word is not easy to do. "Steinbeckish" isn't a word. Though, "Dickensian" is a word. But "Salingerry" isn't. Yet. Let's try to make "Salingerry" a word.

FUN FACT

Queen Victoria loved to belch the alphabet.

Charles Dickens – If your dream dinner party falls on or around December 25th and you're into it, why not invite Charles Dickens to your dream dinner party and ask him to read *A Christmas Carol* to the group? You can also tell him that "Dickensian" has become a word which means reminiscent of the novels of Charles Dickens, especially in suggesting the poor social conditions or comically repulsive characters they portray.

James Baldwin – Who better to shed some much-needed light on the intricacies of race, class, gender, and sexual orientation than this guy. He smoked so be aware of that.

Jane Austen – If you love her novels and are into that era and the whole dresses and Victorian era and stuff, then you would love to dine with her.
Albert Camus – Great appeal for French people, philosophers, and readers. This guy won the Nobel prize in literature. A dinner party with three Nobel prize winners would be cool, though bearing in mind, any meeting with multiple Nobel Prize recipients will inevitably end with the laureates laying their penises on the table to measure to see whose is biggest.

Frederick Douglass – I would be into this. If your purpose in throwing a dream dinner party is to be inspired, then this guy could surely do it.
J.K. Rowling – She's still alive so you could probably just call her agent and have dinner with her anytime. She's also very prolific on Twitter, so you can get a good idea of who she is that way too (for better or for worse).

Harper Lee – Notably reclusive for most of her life and nearly all of her post-*To Kill a Mockingbird* life, dinner with her could be very enlightening. Certainly, everything you hear will be brand new as she has never said it before. And for those who have loved *To Kill a Mockingbird*, asking questions about its origins, inspirations, evolution, and the process in which she engaged in writing it would be fascinating. As would her friendship with Truman Capote.

Gabriel Garcia Marquez – I have tried to read *One Hundred Years of Solitude* numerous times and just can't get into it. If you can and have gotten into it, and find Marquez sufficiently intriguing to invite to your dream dinner party, then by all means, go for it.

PRO TIP

RFK and Harriet Tubman have this thing where it's like there's this joke that only they are in on. It's cute, but after a while it's like, "Could you join us, please?"

John Steinbeck – I would reserve this guy for Steinbeck and literature enthusiasts. Though putting him in the same room as Oprah and letting her tell him what happened when she chose *East of Eden* for her book club could be fun.

Music

The key to determining if you should invite any musicians to your dream dinner party will be answering a few fundamental questions at the outset.

> What is the availability of instruments and microphones and other music-making accoutrements? You are responsible for these yourself.

> Inviting Jimi Hendrix to your dream dinner party sounds like a wonderful idea until everyone realizes that there is no guitar available and George Washington, Gandhi, and Jimi Hendrix are stuck together for an entire meal. Or inviting Pablo Casals to your dream dinner party only to discover that there is no cello on hand; or inviting Jean-Pierre Rampal to your dream dinner party and learning that there is no flute on the premises and all the flute stores are closed. Imagine inviting Sergei Rachmaninoff to your dream dinner party only to have him have to play the spoons because there is no piano. What a waste of a dream dinner party guest.

> How enthusiastically, if at all, will the musician perform pre- and/or post-dinner?

> Is a performance assumed? Yes. Guests know why they are there. While you can't force Karen Carpenter to sing at your dinner party, rest assured she will do so pretty enthusiastically. All these singers typically do. It's called reciprocity. You'll get to pick the songs and the accompaniment and everything.

Can you record them? And if so, would those recordings survive a deceased dream dinner party guest's return to the afterlife? Yes.

Neither John Lennon nor Paul McCartney would independently make my list of dream dinner party guests. However, I might be tempted to include them on my dream dinner party guest list if I were able to record them singing and then sell/distribute the subsequent video. I'd be a billionaire. While the nature of Paul and John's relationship at the time of John's demise is unclear, if they showed up to dinner rest assured they would cooperate.

Mozart – I guess. Though, if you invite Mozart to your dream dinner party and some old guy shows up dressed in Mozarty classical composer clothing, would you be able to say, "You're not Mozart! You're an imposter dressed up in Mozarty clothes and you just want to crash my dream dinner party!" I wouldn't. Like, are there any pictures of Mozart? And how do you prove you *are* Mozart? Like, play some Mozart on the piano? That can't be hard – like, it's Mozart. Doesn't anyone who plays the piano know how to play some Mozart? That being said, inviting Mozart to your dream dinner party, inviting him to gobble down some Bratwurst or Vienna sausage, and then escorting him into your den to compose a new Mozart sonata is not a bad idea. Pairing Mozart with Eminem or Kurt Cobain could be fun.

Lizzo – Yes. She brings her flute everywhere so she could play the flute for you. And always delivers a positive, affirming message. She would by her mere presence make everyone feel good.

George Gershwin – Did you know George Gershwin died when he was only 39? Again, a dream dinner party guest who would be elated to see how his work has evolved and insinuated itself into the canon following his death. For those who love *Rhapsody in Blue, An American in Paris,* and/or *Porgy and Bess* this is a solid choice.

Jim Morrison – I bet he would be fun.

Toni Braxton – An outlier, but she always comes prepared to wow. And you can even specify that she wear that one piece white leather pantsuit she wore in the "You're Making Me High" video, the one with the boots attached.

Jerry Garcia – There are many for whom getting high and eating and playing guitar with Jerry Garcia would be the very apex of cool. I get it. And if you're a dead head, and there do not seem to be degrees of dead headedness—you either are you are not—then by all means, invite him. Imagine the stories, imagine the great melodies, imagine the money you'd get from ticket sales!

Bruce Springsteen – Have you ever met a huge Springsteen fan? The ones who shelled out thousands to see him on Broadway and have seen numerous live shows and compare set lists for shows? There are lots of huge Springsteen fans out there. If you count yourself among them, then selecting Bruce becomes a foregone conclusion. If you are just a regular Springsteen fan, and can get confirmation that you can demand that your dream dinner party guests perform, then selecting Bruce becomes, while not quite a foregone conclusion, certainly more interesting. Inviting Bruce and John Steinbeck and Woody Guthrie would be a great combination for idealists and populists. Surely, idealists and populists wouldn't be concerned with cashing in on a new Springsteen recording. Bruce wrote an in-depth and highly confessional memoir in 2015, where he chronicled intimate details regarding depression and difficult family relationships. How much more could there be to learn?

Prince – Any dinner with Prince will surely end in some sort of fornication. If you invite Prince to your dream dinner party, be prepared to fornicate with him as he loves to fornicate and people are rendered powerless to resist his seduction skills. Ask guests to sign a waiver saying that they agree to fornicate with Prince. Downside, he was also a Jehovah's Witness and will likely want to talk about that. Try to make any fornication last long enough that he won't be able to proselytize.

Paul McCartney – For all the reasons to invite John Lennon, but since he's still alive, you could theoretically dine with him any time. Inadvisable. Also, I don't like to gossip, but I heard he can be a bit self-centered.

Freddie Mercury – This guy is having a well-deserved moment since the release of the Bohemian Rhapsody movie. Anyone interested in having one of the greatest lead singers in the history of rock music at his or her dream dinner party could do no better than Freddie. Imagine Freddie, Robert Plant, and Axl Rose singing together at your dream dinner party. Freddie has also evolved into a hero to gay men, Indians, anyone who loves a good four-octave vocal range, anyone who loves a good comeback story, and anyone who wants to recreate the most memorable performance of Live-Aid at their dream diner party.

Frank Sinatra – I know many Italians who would put him at the top of their list. To dine with and/or get serenaded by Sinatra would be a dream come true for many. Pairs well with JFK, Dean Martin, Ava Gardner, Sammy Davis Jr., Peter Lawford, Marilyn Monroe, Angie Dickinson, Joey Bishop. All the more appealing if you can specify the location and era of your dream dinner party. Imagine dining with Sinatra, Sammy Davis Jr., and some gangster in 1950s Las Vegas. Or with Sinatra, JFK, and Marilyn Monroe in the White House in 1962.

Johnny Cash – This guy is likely tops for anyone who loves country music. He would add a certain gravity to any dream dinner party. Be careful with the music selections for your dream dinner party. Playing his music might be deemed obsequious and depressing. Playing new country music could be disorienting. But what might Johnny Cash think of country music today?

Karen Carpenter – I grew up listening to Karen Carpenter, so she has a soft spot in my heart. Witnessing a Richard and Karen Carpenter reunion would be really poignant. But then you are left with a third dream dinner party spot, and then who to invite? Anne Murray? That won't do. Carole King? Maybe. I think any deceased singer would be elated to come back and know their songs are still being listened to.

> **EAT ME!**
>
> Bruce Spring-roll-steen
>
> This is that thing of when you host a dinner party and you make spring rolls, but instead of adding Chinese stuff like cabbage and shrimp, you add American stuff like apple pie and hot dogs.

Michael Jackson – While not as popular as he once was, Michael Jackson still ranks rather high on our scientific poll of dream dinner party guest respondents. These are people who either do not believe or do not care about the pedophilia allegations. Another negative here, in addition to the pedophilia, is the fact that you might not know which Michael Jackson you are going to get. "ABC" Michael Jackson won't be able to teach you that move they did in *Smooth Criminal* with the leaning. That was so cool.

Elvis Presley – A huge Elvis fan—though I think "huge Elvis fan" is redundant as every Elvis fan seems to be a huge one— would likely want him to sing for the dream dinner party guests, probably do that hip gyration thing, and then stop to croon "I Can't Help Falling in Love With You" tenderly on one knee. A fan like this would not care if they

> **EAT ME!**
>
> Freddie Mercury Tainted Fish
>
> This is that thing of when you host a dinner party and catch a fish in a highly-polluted United States freshwater stream, and you make sure it is highly contaminated with mercury, and then you cook it while singing "We Will Rock You."

got young Elvis or fat Elvis, Army Elvis or *Blue Hawaii* Elvis, green Elvis, skinny Elvis, cold Elvis, hot Elvis, tepid Elvis, ordinary Elvis, illiterate Elvis, erudite Elvis, Las Vegas Elvis, outer space Elvis, farm boy Elvis, beachy Elvis, or any other Elvis that might happen. They just want an Elvis. Undiluted, unabashed, unashamed hagiographic worship would likely be a sufficient goal. But recording a duet with Elvis, either with themselves or another dream dinner party guest, would have its benefits. You could also get the narrative on so many Elvissy things from Elvis himself. What was it like working with his costars? What was your childhood like?

Buddy Holly – Just because he died so young. Come back and live a little more. Or say thank you; especially if you are named Peggy Sue. Or tell him about how you met your spouse at a sock hop while dancing to "Everyday."

Janis Joplin – Just because she died so young too. But also because showing her YouTube videos of Pat Benatar, Courtney Love, the Breeders, Debbie Harry, Tina Turner and telling her that much of that splendor is due in large measure to her.

Eddie Van Halen – So many dudes from my high school revered this guy. I suspect they still do. So if you are a guy from my high school who was super into Eddie Van Halen, go ahead and invite him to your dream dinner party. While dead, he died late enough to know that his contributions to music would live forever.

Kurt Cobain – For children of the 1990s, this is a clear choice. I also wonder what might happen if Janis Joplin, Kurt Cobain, and Jim Morrison got together to sing a song.

MUSICIANS PEOPLE IN MY HIGH SCHOOL LIKED THE MOST:

- Ozzy Osbourne
- all the members of Def Leppard
- that guy from Rush
- all the members of Judas Priest
- the members of Dokken
- that guy from Whitesnake
- Eddie Van Halen
- Randy Rhoads
- anyone from AC/DC, Pink Floyd, or Zeppelin.

Patsy Cline – The queen of country music would be a great guest for fans of country music. Keep windows closed, though. Once a bird flew into a dream dinner party she was at and she flipped her wig.

Aretha Franklin – She is always a fun time. Sometimes she can be a little hesitant to sing "R-E-S-P-E-C-T" but can be persuaded.

FAVORITE DRINKS OF MUSICIANS YOU MAY WISH TO INVITE:

- Beyonce: Long Island iced tea
- Bono: Jack Daniels
- Lady Gaga: Jameson on the rocks
- Madonna: Pomegranate martini
- Slash: Jack Daniels
- Sting: Jack Daniels
- Taylor Swift: Whiskey sour

Judy Garland – I like this one. I like it for a number of reasons. Judy could have used a hug. Invite her to your dream dinner party and give her a hug. Also, starting a dream dinner party with Judy Garland singing "Somewhere Over the Rainbow" would be astonishing. Though, if you also have, like, Ponce de Leon at your dream dinner party, explaining to Ponce de Leon who Judy Garland is would require a great deal of energy. Though, you would get to say, "Ponce. Judy. Judy. Ponce," during introductions.

Barbra Streisand – I like this one, too, for the huge Streisand fan. And any huge

Streisand fan knows that she will likely require a complex meal of just the right grains and vegetables and need it served at just the right temperature. She will also likely need to bring her cloned Coton de Tulear dogs, so be sure not to invite any other dream dinner party guests who might have dog allergies.

Beethoven – Not a lot of bang for your buck here. Leave this one for classical music people. Tempted to take a selfie with Beethoven? I bet 100% of the people to whom you show that selfie will think Beethoven is your great uncle dressed up in an Oktoberfest or Confederate soldier uniform.

Whitney Houston – Oh, Whitney Whitney Whitney. Just be sure to specify which one you want. I've had clients have a wonderful time with SuperBowl 1991 Whitney. Be careful with whom you sit her though. While seating her next to Beyonce or Aretha might seem like a good idea, it can also foster competition.

Sting – No. Big no. He is right up there with Mother Teresa and Tom Hanks as dream dinner party guests to avoid. Again, I don't like to gossip, but this one time, Sting slept over at a dream dinner party because he was too drunk to get home. My friend was in the kitchen making coffee in the morning, and Sting came up the basement stairs into the kitchen wearing nothing but his underwear. He didn't say anything to my friend, he just shuffled past and went back into the spare bedroom. My friend was curious what he was doing down there, so he ventured downstairs to check it out. It turns out that in his drunken state, Sting couldn't find either one of the bathrooms upstairs on the main level, so he went into the basement and shit beneath the stairs all over the floor. My friend told Sting that he had to clean up his shit. That's when Sting decided to use the clean bath towels to smear his shit all over the basement floor, then he just tossed the towels into the laundry tub. One good thing did come out of it, though. We now get to say "Sting shit the basement drunk" as the top of the drunkenness meter

Beyonce – Obviously.

Shakira – This one can do it all. And how fun to reenact her Superbowl halftime show. See, J.Lo.

J.Lo. – This one can do it all. And how fun to reenact her Superbowl halftime show. See, Shakira.

Celine Dion – Imagine having dinner aboard a cruise ship while Celine Dion sings "My Heart Will Go On" to you. For added bonus, you can invite the old lady who threw the necklace into the water.

Bono – I understand this. To some he would be inspiring, like Gandhi. To some, he is a rock legend and would make a perfect guest for all the reasons you'd want to dine with a rock legend. Some Irish folks might want to assemble a Who's Who of Ireland and serve corned beef and cabbage and potatoes for the dream dinner party. Who else to include? St. Patrick himself. JFK. Bono. Eminem. – No. It just wouldn't end well, it seems.

Television

Much of this will depend on individual taste. I can't advise you to invite Carroll O'Connor to your dream dinner party unless you are a huge *All in the Family* fan. Or a huge fan of *In the Heat of the Night*, which ran on NBC and CBS from 1987 to 1994. Or a huge bigot who is highly confused and thinks Archie Bunker is a real person. Though, I can see how anyone really invested in the medium of television would want to converse with Carroll O'Connor, as he portrayed one of the most memorable characters in all of television. There are also those who transcend TV, like Lucille Ball and Johnny Carson, who, while they are television actors, have also insinuated themselves into our collective cultural consciousness.

This category is also fertile ground for those who just wish to have fun. Imagine Amy Schumer and Bob Newhart and Jackie Gleason cracking jokes as they eat together. This category is also fertile ground for those susceptible to what's hot right now. So be careful.

Lucille Ball – This could either be really fun or really sad. Though, just finding out if it's really fun or really sad might be the goal, or at least part of the fun. Lucille died in April of 1989 and smoked Chesterfields until the day she died so, like deceased movie stars, when she arrives at your dream dinner party, she will likely expect a fresh carton of Chesterfields and ash trays and, not having experienced the changing mores of the last three decades, expect to smoke at and throughout your entire dream dinner party. Telling her she can't likely does not end well.

Johnny Carson – If you're into him, then why not? But in this expert's opinion, he doesn't really DO anything, does he? He just had people on his show who did stuff. That said, if you want some inside scoop on LOTS of people, then there might be no one better than this guy.

The cast of *The Facts of Life* – Obviously Charlotte Rae, Nancy McKeon, Lisa Whelchel, Kim Fields, and Mindy Cohn, better known as Edna Garrett, Jo Polniaczek, Blair Warner, Tootie, and Natalie, respectively, should be at the top of everyone's list, should you be able to negotiate them as one guest. If not, inviting just three of them without the others will be awkward. Oh, what fun you would have reminiscing about the days at Eastland Academy and later, as boarders above Miss Garrett's bakery shop, Edna's Edibles.

Bernie Mac – I watched *Ocean's 11* recently and said to myself, "I really miss Bernie Mac." I always associate him with *The Bernie Mac Show* and the HBO comedy specials.

Sherman Hemsley – If you loved *The Jeffersons* or love dry cleaners, then this is an obvious choice

Mary Tyler Moore – Reenacting the opening sequence from *The Mary Tyler Moore Show* with Mary Tyler Moore would be very fun. You'd have to host your dream dinner party in Minneapolis though. People into Minneapolis could invite her, Prince, and Louis Hennepin. Or have her have a clumsy-off with Lucille Ball.

Leonard Nimoy – There is a certain *faction* of people who would love Mr. Spock to narrate their dream dinner party. This *faction* of people would probably also invite William Shatner and George Takkei. Which is fine. Everyone needs something.

Michael Landon – This is risky. You invite Michael Landon expecting Pa Ingalls, and what if when he shows up at your dream dinner party, he hits on your newly resurrected grandma? And she's into him? And they leave your dream dinner party to go do it on your twin bed? I've heard that Michael Landon could be a little "handsy", if you know what I mean.

WAYS TO SAY WHAT TEEN BOYS DID UNDERNEATH THEIR ICONIC RED BATHING SUITED FARRAH FAWCETT MEXICAN BLANKET POSTER:

- Shaking hands with the milkman
- Manual override
- Marching the penguin
- Polishing the banister
- Lone Rangering
- Boxing the one-eyed champ
- Celebrating Palm Sunday
- Visiting the safety deposit box
- Finding Nemo
- Dialing the rotary phone
- Turning on the sprinklers
- Spearing the bearded clam
- Dating Pamela Handerson
- Paddling the pink canoe
- Scratching Yoda behind the ears
- Battling the purple headed yogurt slinger
- Taking selfies at the Bean
- Going to the palm prom
- Burping the worm
- Tapping into your potential
- Playing closet Frisbee
- Cuddling the kielbasa
- Flipping your omelet
- Looking for clues with Fred and Daphne
- Making chowder with Sailor Ned
- Sailing the mayonnaise seas
- Shaking hands with Lincoln
- Rubbing Rob Reiner
- Keynoting in Cupertino

Farrah Fawcett – There are likely hundreds of thousands of young men who learned to beat their meat (or whatever you call it (See Appendix D)) while relaxing underneath Farrah's iconic Mexican blanket poster with her iconic red bathing suit and her iconic nipples who would like to invite Ms. Fawcett to their dream dinner party to thank her for all the good times.

Fred Rogers – He's having a moment—following 2018's *Won't You Be My Neighbor?* documentary and 2019's *A Beautiful Day in the Neighborhood* feature film starring Tom Hanks. You can invite him if it'll make you feel good. Don't expect to curse or make fun of people without getting some sort of lesson on kindness. Might be a buzzkill.

Jerry Seinfeld – No. He would drive up to your house in one of his fancy cars and demand tons of attention.

Jim Henson – This would be like having all the Muppets with you at the dream dinner party. Could be fun.

Candice Bergen – It's easy to forget what a huge deal Murphy Brown was in the early 1990s.

PRO TIP

Be sure to clearly annunciate that you want "Mr. Spock" at your dream dinner party. Dr. Spock was a famous child pediatrician. So, unless you want to spend a dream dinner party talking about psychoanalysis in children, speak clearly.

Cast of *Saturday Night Live*/ Lorne Michaels – Paying homage to the creator and/or any cast member of *Saturday Night Live* by inviting them to your dream dinner party is a sound use of a dream dinner party invite. For some, recreating favorite SNL skits with real, actual SNL stars would be one of the best and most fun ways to spend an evening imaginable.

Carroll O'Connor – I suspect some xenophobes will invite Carroll O'Connor to their dream dinner party expecting Archie Bunker and be disappointed.

Issa Rae – Her journey from YouTube star to HBO powerhouse would be incredible to hear. And she'd be fun.

Jackie Gleason – This is the guy who threatened his wife with domestic violence for laughs, right? There are those who would revel in inviting him to a dream dinner party just to school him about how people treat each other in the 21st century. Seems perfectly legitimate.

Oprah Winfrey – This one could be a real triple threat—a business leader, a television star, and a vocal civil rights advocate. The trouble with Oprah is, so long as she is still alive, there are better choices, since you could ostensibly win a dinner with Oprah any time. Decide which facet of Oprah you wish to explore. Business leader? Black woman business leader? TV star? That said, Oprah would be very fun.

Andy Griffith – Can't see this guy being much fun. But if you are into geriatric television stars, then you probably can't do much better than the Andy Griffith, Angela Lansbury, Wilford Brimley combination.

Walter Cronkite – I like this one. Journalists and historians alike would benefit from an in-depth and personal conversation with him.

Bob Hope – I never got why this guy was even famous. Or why anyone liked him. Skip him.

Michael J. Fox – One of the 80s most-loved TV and movie stars evolved into both an inspiration and a crusader. And the *Back to the Future* trilogy stands the test of time.

Alan Alda – For *M*A*S*H* devotees, what could be better than having Hawkeye Pierce at their dream dinner party? *M*A*S*H* was a huge deal. 125 million people watched its finale, billed as a television movie, on February 28, 1983, making it the highest-rated single television episode of all time.

David Letterman – Holds vast appeal for comedians and Indianans.

Julia Child – Any "foodie" would likely enjoy cooking their own dream dinner party meal with Julia Child.

Ed Sullivan – The only insight you might be able to get from this guy is what the Beatles were like prior to shooting the February 9, 1964 episode of *The Ed Sullivan Show*.

Bob Newhart – A staple of television for decades and the creator of several TV shows often listed among the "Best Ever." He also embodies a certain brand of observational humor that has inspired many of today's top comedians.

Edward R. Murrow – A journalist who would surely be astonished at the state of both the world and journalism today. Journalists eager for inspiration at what must be a very difficult time for their profession would get a jolt of inspiration from dining with this man.

Gary Coleman – I can understand the need to give this man, who gave us Gen Xers so many laughs as kids, a dinner to say thanks. And if he happens to record a "Whatchu talkin' bout Willis?" as your outgoing voicemail message, then so be it.

Walter White and Jesse Pinkman – How awesome would this be? Not only could they cook you a batch of grade-A blue crystal meth, but they would be so fun to hang out with, and you could ask Jesse Pinkman to record, "This is my own personal domicile, and I will not be harassed, bitch." For when people

FOR ALL YOU PHILISTINES...

Ten Most Watched Television Shows of the 1980s:

- *60 Minutes*
- *Dallas*
- *The Cosby Show*
- *Cheers*
- *Murder, She Wrote*
- *The Golden Girls*
- *NFL Monday Night Football*
- *Dynasty*
- *Who's the Boss?*
- *Family Ties.*

FUN FACT

Because he was so very fond of pancakes, bacon, and bagels with cream cheese and lox, Leonardo da Vinci often enjoyed breakfast for dinner. In fact, he painted the Mona Lisa at one of these breakfasts for dinner. Much of the luminescence around Mona Lisa's bosoms is created not from paint, but from bacon grease.

ring your doorbell.

Casts – If you are that into television that you would want to offer a spot at your dream dinner party to a television actor, then it stands to reasons that there's a show you love so much that you would want several members of that show's cast to attend your dream dinner party. Start thinking about which two or three members of your favorite show you would want. How to select your favorite two cast members of *The Wire* or *The Sopranos?*

Sample dialogue:

> **Jerry Seinfeld:** What is the deal with dream dinner parties?

> **Jim Henson (as Kermit):** You're asking me? I'm a frog.

> **Jerry Seinfeld:** Well that's just it, I wasn't asking you. I was positing it in a rhetorical manner. As the start of a bit.

> **Jim Henson (as Kermit):** (Singing. To great applause.) Movin' right along, footloose and fancy-free. Getting there is half the fun, come share it with me. I'm a frog.

> **Jerry Seinfeld:** Right. You've mentioned that. Anyway. I'll get back to my bit.

> **Jim Henson (as Kermit):** If you hadn't left the swamp, you'd be feeling pretty miserable anyhow.

> **Jerry Seinfeld:** I didn't come from a swamp. Look, I really don't want any trouble.

> **Jim Henson (as the Swedish Chef):** We don't want any trouble either. Let me give you some of my meatballs to really get this dream dinner party going.

Jerry Seinfeld: I was supposed to headline. I will get the dream dinner party started.

They sit silently as Jerry Seinfled regroups. After a while:

Jim Henson (as Kermit): Fuck. This sucks.

Jerry Seinfeld: What the fuck did you just say to me?

Jim Henson (as the Swedish Chef): I didn't say anything to you, bro.

Jerry Seinfeld: Well I know you didn't. And I'm not your bro. The other one did – the monkey one.

Jim Henson (as the Swedish Chef): That's Kermit.

Jerry Seinfeld: Tell Kermit I'm going to kick his ass.

Painters

Given the price of paintings these days, inviting a painter to your dream dinner party could be not only interesting but also highly profitable. Even if you have some aversion to doing that parasitic thing where you get them to paint on a canvas to sell it, give them a bunch of paint and some brushes and tell them to go nuts on your dining room. That would be incredible. I would also love to watch a painter paint. Especially the abstract expressionists.

Leonardo da Vinci – In 2017, Prince Badr bin Abdullah bought da Vinci's "Salvator Mundi" for $450.3 million. It is currently on display on Arabian Crown

Prince Mohammed bin Salman's luxury yacht. How long did it take da Vinci to paint that? You think he could knock another one out in the time allotted for a dream dinner party? Or is it the age of "Salvator Mundi" that makes it so valuable? What would a brand-new stick figure painting from Leonardo da Vinci go for?

Pablo Picasso – I don't like to gossip, but I heard that this guy could get a little "handsy" at times. Especially after a few glasses of absinthe. Also, did you know his given name was Pablo Diego José Francisco de Paula Juan Nepomuceno María de los Remedios Cipriano de la Santísima Trinidad Ruiz y Picasso?

FUN FACT

Frieda Kahlo can do that thing of when you pull the tablecloth off the table with all the dishes on it and the dishes and all the food stays put.

Michelangelo di Lodovico Buonarroti Simoni – I guess. Whatever. He loves shrimp. And keg stands. And practical jokes. But from what I understand, he's the sort of practical joker who will rub turkey juice on all the vegetarians' plates. Weird stuff like that.

FUN FACT

Mark Rothko – I would love to watch him paint something. He paints those paintings that make you say, "I could totally do that!" but then you try to do that and your painting just doesn't look like a Rothko. How did he do it? How did he choose those colors? He also killed himself. Why?

Vincent Van Gogh's favorite condiment was mustard.

Vincent Van Gogh – If you can have some sort of assurance that he'd be willing, then you could invite this guy to your dream dinner party, give him some paintbrushes and a canvas and some paints, and then let him do his thing while, you eat and you're set for life. It would also be interesting to watch him work. He also had an interesting life. Make sure you don't need a translator though.

Georgia O'Keefe – This woman's story is really inspiring. From New York, where her husband Arthur Stieglitz cheated on her, to Santa Fe, where she flourished as a painter and then left the bulk of her estate to her young male caretaker when she died in 1986. Also, she painted vaginas.

Frida Kahlo – The advantages of inviting her to your dream dinner party are threefold. I bet she is one heck of a storyteller and has some really great tales to tell. She could also paint you something for you to either cherish or sell at

Sotheby's at the end of the dinner. She also seems like the type of person who if you said, "I love that cloak, Frida" she'd be all "Here, you can have it" and then you'd get a new cloak too. And you could walk around and when people say, "I love your cloak" you could say, "Thanks. Frida Kahlo gave it to me."

BREAKING THE ICE

Georgie O'Keeffe

DO ask: Where did you summon the audacity to integrate modernism, surrealism, and precisionism to create what is uniquely your own style? Do you have a favorite painting?

DON'T ask: What is the deal with all the vaginas?

Jacob Lawrence – Seeing him, a great storyteller of the ordinary lives of black people, see what ordinary life looks like now would be incredible.

Andy Warhol – Expect the unexpected when you invite Warhol to your dream dinner party. That's all I have to say!

Keith Haring – I like this one. He died way too soon. And he seems like the sort of guy who, if asked nicely, would paint his signature squiggles wherever you asked him. As someone who died way too soon from complications from the HIV virus, I might be tempted to give him the drugs available today to see if we could postpone his demise.

Banksy – Just finding out who this guy is might be worth expending a dream dinner party invitation spot for some. Though I would caution those of you who would like to invite Banksy to their dream dinner party just for the sake of exposing his identity and cashing in on such exposure. That is not cool; and there would be easier ways to make money from the dream dinner party that are far less nefarious. Additionally, inviting him (or her—do we *know* that Banksy is a man, or do we just assume he is?) to your dream dinner party presumes that *someone* knows who he is.

Banksy: My main goal as an artist is to maintain my anonymity.

Literally Every Other Artist: My main goal as artist is to be fa

mous.

Banksy: Even as an anonymous person, my works still sell for tens of millions of dollars.

Literally Every Other Artist: Eat shit, Bansky.

The Julias

So many Julias from which to choose. You can never go wrong with any of these Julias.

Julia Child – To help you cook.

Julia Roberts – To add some glamour.

Julia Louis-Dreyfus – To make you laugh. And make cursing sophisticated.

Julia Ward Howe – To sing her famous song "Battle Hymn of the Republic for You"

Julia Alvarez – To read from her novel, "How the Garcia Girls Lost Their Accents"

Julia Garner – for *Ozark* fans.

The Athletes

There are several plausible and wholly legitimate reasons to select an athlete or group of athletes. Everyone who has a favorite team, a favorite player, a favorite play, memory, championship, goal, dunk, homer, ace, or anything else sportsy should consider an athlete at a dream dinner party. Though, know that the tactic of answering "I'm inviting Soren Kierkegaard, Stephen Hawking, and the Gronk to my dream dinner party. Can you even imagine the arguments they'll have?" won;'t work that well here.

Accolades. Somewhere there is a someone who yearns to dine with Don Bart-lett, Steve Gould, and Bill Grant. These three, obviously, are the top three Canadian curlers in Canadian curling history. Somewhere, there is an aspiring curler whose dream dinner party would necessarily include these three—for inspiration, for tips, for stories from the golden days of curling. Somewhere there is a someone who yearns to dine with Ted Williams, Carl Yastrzemski, and Nomar Garciaparra, three of the best Red Sox in history. The same is true of fans of the New York Yankees, the Milwaukee Brewers, Houston Astros, Cleveland Indians, Cleveland Browns, Dallas Cowboys, New England Patriots, Boston Bruins, Chicago Blackhawks, Chicago Bulls, New York Knicks, and Boston Celtics. And every other team in the NBA, MLB, NFL, NHL, WNBA, etc. And I don't even know about soccer teams. Surely, the very nature of fandom necessarily includes the idea that your fandom is the purest, largest, most intense fandom of all the fans. But somewhere, the biggest fan for any endeavor from professional sports to tennis to golf to rowing to archery to downhill skiing to bobsledding, exists and to him or her, selecting their three dream dinner party guests would be easy.

Curiosity. Do we really know how it feels to fall at the Olympics or suffer the sort of disappointment experienced by Buffalo Bills kicker Scott Norwood or Red Sox first baseman Bill Buckner, or endured a career ending injury with millions watching like Joe Theisman? Or how it truly felt to be a member of the 1980 U.S. Olympic hockey team, any of Michael Jordan's game winning shots, Jesse Owens' 1936 Olympics appearance, Jackie Robinson's first

ALLERGIES OF ATHLETES YOU MAY WISH TO INVITE:

- Serena Williams: Peanuts
- Drew Brees: Gluten
- Tiger Woods: Pollen

game, Muhammad Ali's win against George Foreman in 1974, the Patriots' comeback in SuperBowl LI. It's likely there is sufficient literature, interview snippets, analysis, and footage to satiate the average individual. A true "biggest" fan will want a dream dinner party to interrogate, investigate, evaluate, and otherwise scrutinize the sources of their greatest defeats or triumphs.

Set up a competition. Once you receive verification that you can host your dream dinner party anywhere—any basketball court, any ice-skating rink, any baseball diamond, tennis court, golf course, ski slope, or pool—and once you've received verification that you can demand your guests do what you tell them to, and once you've verified that your dream dinner party guests are arriving at your dream dinner party in their physical prime, it's time to set up a dream dinner party skirmish. Could Ted Williams or Wade Boggs get a hit off Nolan Ryan or Greg Maddux? What happens when Roger Federer and Rod Laver have a singles match? Or a doubles match against Arthur Ashe and John McEnroe? What is the result of Tiger Woods playing golf with Arnold Palmer?

The host inserting him or herself into the action is the point here. To set up a match between you (the host of the dream dinner party) and the invitee(s). How would it feel to be the 4th in a tennis doubles match with McEnroe, Ashe, and Laver? Or to pitch to Babe Ruth? Or to try to catch a pass from Tom Brady or Johnny Unitas? Or to goaltend while Wayne Gretzky shoots pucks at you? Or to play ping pong against Ma Long, Zhang Jike, or Liu Guolang? However, this could be embarrassing for you. It might be a good idea to see if, under the stipulations of your dream dinner party, you are allowed to bestow yourself with athletic ability.

Money. You can charge admission to the above, and/or film it and sell it to ESPN. You can also invite current professional players to the dream dinner party and invite them to throw future games. This seems highly illegal and highly unreliable, and there are easier ways to make money from the dream dinner party. Or you could "Tonya Harding" the living invitees to your dream dinner party. Which means you'd be inviting an opponent to the dream dinner party, which feels malicious and not in the spirit of the dream dinner party process.

Michael Jordan – This guy checks so many boxes, for Chicago natives, for North Carolina fans, for golfers, for business tycoons. There also seems to be a perpetual, long-standing, and really pointless conversation about who is the best basketball player ever, LeBron in his prime, Michael Jordan in his prime, Kobe Bryant in his prime, or Magic Johnson in his prime. Or whomever else [insert favorite NBA Player here] in their prime. I say the conversation is inevitably pointless because there are those who place greater weight on championships and those who place greater emphasis on statistics; those who discount a player's value because of the presence of great teammates and those who posit that a player's greatness should be augmented as he made his teammates greater. Inviting three players in this "who was better in their prime?" conversation, identifying a

This "who is the greatest ever" analysis seems to be an omnipresent and alluring discourse for fans of all sports. Even those heavily reliant on statistics, like sprinting, could be reanalyzed with everyone wearing the same aerodynamic leotard and supersonic sneakers; especially when the fastest person ever is a difference of less than 0.25 of a second. As such, the above Michael Jordan analysis can be transferred, employed, or otherwise utilized for any other athlete. Invite Jesse Owens, Carl Lewis, and Usain Bolt to dinner, make them race before you start serving appetizers; or Serena Williams, Martina Navratilova, and Steffi Graf. You can join them for doubles. Or try to his off Roger Clemons, Greg Maddux, and Pedro Martinez; or Pele, Cristiano Ronaldo, and Lionel Messi. There is also a temptation to reunite teammates who achieved greatness. Inviting Michael Jordan, BJ Armstrong, and Scottie Pippin and reminiscing with them would be fun. If you never got to see them live – or if you did get to see them play live and want to replicate that feeling – then why not. You can also do Michael Jordan, Dennis Rodman, and Steve Kerr; or Michael Jordan, Dennis Rodman, And Kim Jong Un.

Jim Brown – Cleveland fans could reunite him with his 1964 Championship coach Blanton Collier and teammate quarterback Frank Ryan. Or invite him with Barry Sanders and Walter Payton to see who can running back the best. Arthur Ashe – Let him know they named the U.S. Open stadium after him. Try to return his serve. Tell him all about Venus and Serena Williams.

Tom Landry – Show him what New England Patriots head coach Bill Belichick wears on the sidelines, and he will flip his wig. Invite Jerry Jones to the dream dinner party also.

Joe DiMaggio – Appeals to Yankees fans. Could pair well with some of the other Yankees of his era for an impromptu baseball game in your back yard, or with Marilyn Monroe for an immersive conversation about their marriage. Invite Jeter, Rodriguez, or Mattingly to join him.

Babe Ruth – This could be interesting. If you are a big fan of his and want to resurrect his less-than-stellar reputation, inviting him to a dream dinner party would be a good way to do so. What if he's super erudite and the rumors abounding about his gluttony and infidelity and overarching poor character are all made up by a Red Sox fan? You also run the risk of him being just the sort of pig he's portrayed as and ruining your dream dinner party.

EAT ME!

Jim Apple Brown Betty

This is that thing of when you host a dinner party and make a dessert like apple crisp, and then you run it to the table while your guests try to tackle you.

Simone Biles – If you watched the 2021 Summer Olympics in Tokyo from your La-Z-Boy and had an opinion about Simone Biles withdrawing from a competition because, in addition to having the "twisties," she needed to address some mental health challenges, now is the time to invite her into your living room and tell her so.

Lou Gehrig – Another two-fer, an inspirational story and a great baseball player. But be prepared for some disappointment when you tell him that he has a really shitty disease named after him.

Ted Williams – The Greatest Hitter Who Ever Lived, the Splendid Splinter, Teddy Ballgame. Any baseball fan would likely want to have the greatest hitter who ever lived at their dream dinner party. The fact that he was a member of the Boston Red Sox for his entire career might dissuade some Yankees fans.

PRO TIP

This one time, Benjamin Franklin came to a friend's dream dinner party. He kept sneaking into the bathroom and snorting Special K. He did so much, he ended up in a near-coma and we had to call the paramedics. After an hour with him outside, he revived enough to refuse the offered ride to the hospital and instead staggered back inside to the bathroom, where he did more Special K, puked, and passed out. Thing is, this was a sushi-making dream dinner party.

Muhammad Ali – Fight him. Just to say you did. Or tell him thanks. He could also pair well with the *One Night in Miami* folks, Malcolm X and Sam Cooke.

Gordie Howe – I don't know a hockey fan who wouldn't love to play a few rounds with this guy.

Vince Lombardi – Watching a modern football game with him would either be exhilarating or depressing. Invite him and Aaron Rodgers just to gauge how Vince Lombardi would feel about him.

Walter Payton – Da Bears. See also, Jim Brown.

Babe Didrikson Zaharias – This woman excelled at everything before turning to golf exclusively. Invite her for dinner, play 18 holes with her beforehand.

Johnny Unitas – You still genuflect when you say his name in Baltimore. If you're form Baltimore, eating crab cakes and drinking Natty Boh with Jonny Unitas, Cal Ripken, and Michael Phelps might just be a dream come true. Or Ray Lewis. Or Brooks Robinson.

Larry Bird – One on one with Larry Bird would be fun for Hoosiers and Bostonians alike.

John McEnroe – How awesome would it be to play a set with John McEnroe before dinner?

Magic Johnson – See Larry Bird but with Los Angeles instead.

Tom Brady – If you don't mind being the second-best looking person in the room, then why not? Invite Peyton Manning and Joe Montana (specifying that you need prime Peyton Manning and prime Joe Montana) and see who the best quarterback is.

Evel Knievel – It is impossible to overstate how big this guy was in the 1970s. Any motorcycle enthusiast would love to have him at their dream dinner party. I suspect that since he is already dead, you could goad him into jumping anything. Film it. Sell it. You know the drill.

The Leaders

There's a reason that *The 7 Habits of Highly Effective People* has sold almost as many copies as this book is going to. People want to know how to be effective. And when asked at what it is they want to be effective, the most succinct response is leadership. I think that leadership is more instinctual than learnable. Like, some people just have "it" and some people just do not have "it." Surely there are skills you can learn, like how you shake hands and how you nod your head and do that thing of when you say, "So what I hear you saying is…" when your underlings talk to you.

Identifying a leader as a dream dinner party guest is a move intended to connote power. Frankly, I think it connotes just the opposite. If you are that into leadership, then why are you asking a leader to lead you?

Of course, just like any other historical figure, sometimes the rationale for inviting the person to your dream dinner is not so much to replicate their experiences, but just to pay homage or engage in some in-depth first-hand intellectual inquiry.

It would also be fun to show these leaders the men and women leading our country today. Their reactions would be enlightening. And embarrassing. Tell

General Douglas MacArthur that leaders were scared of our former POTUS's tweets. He'd be all "Wow—what are these tweets of which you speak?" Then tell him they are 280-character, word salads from a tiny-fingered draft dodger.

George Patton – People into war and strategy-things like that would love this guy, the U.S. Army general who commanded the U.S. Army in France and Germany after the invasion of Normandy. General Patton was not involved in the planning or implementation of the invasion of Normandy, so he would not be able to provide a first-hand account of what happened that day. That day has taken on such a mythical place in the collective consciousness. You could theoretically just say, "I want someone who stormed the beaches at Normandy on D-Day," and he would appear at your dream dinner party table.

Jane Addams - Suffragist, settlement house founder, peace activist and Nobel Peace Prize winner, Jane Addams rejected marriage and motherhood in favor of a lifetime commitment to social reform. Could be just what we need.

Moses – This would either be really cool or a huge disappointment. Like, what if he told you that the parting of the Red Sea never happened? Also, and I don't like to gossip, but I heard he can get a little "handsy" after a few Merlots.

Michelle Obama – This is a tough one. She's still alive. So, theoretically, a dinner party with her as a guest need not be a dream one. But then, what are the chances you might ever be at a dinner where Michelle Obama is attending? And that such a dinner will be sufficiently intimate so that you can talk to her.

Napoleon – Let's just talk about the elephant in the room. And it's not Napoleon's elephant-sized penis. It's Napoleon's teeny weeny peeny. At the outset, it'd be very interesting to have him at your dream dinner party—obtaining first-hand knowledge of what it was like to march back and forth, across and around, and in Europe conquering people. How he approached his battle decisions. How it felt. But then, you'd also have to see his penis, wouldn't you? It was notoriously small. Or maybe that was just a rumor. But if that's the case, how do you conquer Europe and then someone starts a rumor that you have a small penis, and that is the thing that sticks? Wouldn't you be so mad? Like, "Hey. I literally just conquered Europe and a fellow soldier saw me pee and we were doing the Russian invasion and it was cold out so my penis shriveled and it wasn't even just a soldier it was a soldier that I had just disciplined a few days prior because he refused to do something soldiery that I asked him to do." Reuniting Napoleon and Josephine at the dream dinner party would certainly make things exciting.

Harvey Milk – This guy was an American politician and the first openly gay man to be elected to public office in California, as a member of the San Francisco Board of Supervisors. His experience in the counterculture of the

1960s caused him to shed many of his conservative views about individual freedom and the expression of sexuality. He was assassinated by Dan White, another member of the San Francisco Board of Supervisors who had a resigned a few days prior. Invite him with Pete Buttigieg to let him see his impact. Invite him with Sean Penn (who won an Oscar for Best Actor for playing him in the film *Milk*) and have a Milk-Off.

Charlemagne – I don't even know what this guy did. It seems like I was supposed to learn about him in lots of history classes, but I just never did. But yeah, if you're into whatever part of history in which Charlemagne did his thing, then go for it.

Che Guevara – There are a host of lingering questions about how Mr. Guevara reconciled seemingly contrary ethos that he espoused simultaneously. Talking to him about this would be fascinating. Also, getting his reaction to seeing his face on t-shirts would be cool.

Thomas Jefferson – As one of the greatest political minds and one of the architects of democracy, one would expect him to have easily made the top ten. But recent revelations about his relationship with one of the people he enslaved, Sally Hemmings, has tarnished his once-shimmering reputation somewhat.

Franklin Delano Roosevelt – So much to unpack here. I fancy this guy a true and fearless leader. But then with the marital infidelity…it would be a shame to discover that this guy was an asshole, wouldn't it? For World War 2 aficionados, you really can't go wrong with FDR.

Susan B. Anthony – Narrowly missing the top ten, Susan B. Anthony scored higher this year than she ever has before. Women put her on their lists of dream dinner party guests and when asked why, said they would like to pay their respects, say thank you, etc. The 2016 election surely prompted some of this.

Stormy Daniels – Appeals to both women and men for vastly different reasons.

Ruth Bader Ginsburg – I bet you could, with some planning, have your spleen or pancreas or kidney or all of the above removed and have them transplanted into RBG when she arrives at your dream dinner party. Then, she could walk back to SCOTUS and say, "I'm back bitches! I was only sleeping. Now get the fuck outta my chair, Amy." That would be need to be clarified when you are figuring out the metaphysical rules and regulations of the dream dinner party. Though,

PRO TIP

Don't ever tell FDR he has to go outside to smoke.

even if you just have RBG for a few hours, still worth it. And even after the documentary and the books and the memes, I bet there is still so much to learn.

Robert E. Lee – How did it feel to graduate from West Point and then fight for the Confederacy? He was clearly a mastermind and a great leader. What were his feelings? During the war, at Appomattox, after the war? What does he think about the divisions amongst Americans today? Also, showing him that his house in Arlington, VA is still intact and just as he left it, except it now overlooks some of the United States' most hallowed ground would be cool. Pairs well with Ulysses S. Grant.

Sojourner Truth – She was born into slavery in Swartekill, New York and escaped to freedom with her infant daughter in 1826. She was six feet tall, had a powerful voice and driven by deep religious conviction, Truth was an ardent abolitionist and women's rights activist. Among many of Truth's legacies, the tone and substance of her language looms large. She stumped the country speaking on emancipation, politicians, political action, racism, women's rights and segregation. Perhaps her best known speech was the stirring "Ain't I a Woman?" delivered at a women's convention in Ohio in 1851. When Truth died in 1883, her funeral in Battle Creek, Michigan was the largest the town had ever seen, a testimony to how her heroic and courageous life touched so many around her.

Nelson Mandela – If you want a distinguished guest who could regale you and your other guests with tales of grace and dignity and courage, then you can do no better than this guy.

BREAKING THE ICE

Che Guevara

DO ask: How do you reconcile your multiple and contradictory ethos?

DON'T ask: Do you think you look better on the red t-shirts or on the olive green t-shirts?

Andrew Jackson – Ew. Just don't. I bet he smells like scalp. Like, when he takes his hat off, I bet you can smell his scalp. And body odor. And I bet he burps. And eats with his fingers. And likes his steak extra well done.

John Adams – I bet this guy would have so much good intelligence about people. And his infamous feud with Jefferson suggests to me that he is super catty.

Ulysses S. Grant – If you are going to invite Robert E. Lee, then give serious consideration to inviting Grant, as well.

Nikita Khrushchev – He infamously removed his shoe at a United Nations meeting and started banging it on the table. Attention hog much? If you want to pair him with JFK, then that would be cool. Otherwise, what's really the point of him? **EAT ME!**

Czar Nicolas II – I'm not even sure this guy did anything. He's mostly famous because people thought a stranger was his daughter? Yawn.

Margarita Thatcher

This is that thing of when you host a dinner party and for cocktail hour make a margarita, but instead of salt on the rim, you rim the glass with iron-rich foods like liver and spinach.

Harriet Tubman – What was the underground railroad like?

Malcolm X – What would he think about life in the United States in the 21st Century?

Charles De Gaulle – Sure.

Eleanor Roosevelt – Lots of reasons to invite her, one of the greatest women who has ever lived. Sadly, one of the reasons to invite her that springs to mind is to get the scoop on all the infidelity that was happening between FDR and his mistresses and between her and her mistresses.

Winston Churchill – People into WW2 or anglophiles in general, or those eager to host some sort of world leaders summit dream dinner party, can't go wrong with this selection.

Ronald Reagan – Just narrowly missed the top ten. If you get the Reagan who doesn't remember anything at your dream dinner party, then what's really the point? Like, why not just invite a toddler? Getting a definitive statement regarding how he despises certain people today would be fun.

Harry S Truman – An in-depth conversation with him about the decision to drop the atomic bomb would either be positively fascinating or a real disappointment. Like, what if he said, "I flipped a coin."

Marsha P. Johnson – She was a LGBTQ activist and drag queen prominent in New York City's Greenwich Village in the 1960s and instrumental the burgeoning gay-rights movement. Johnson is said to have resisted arrest and thrown the first bottle (or brick or stone) at police during the 1969 Stonewall Riots, which sparked the national LGBTQ movement. Do not invite her to educate someone on how LGBTQ people are people too; invite her to have fun.

Ruby Bridges – I'm into this one. The girl who desegregated the all-white

William Frantz Elementary School in New Orleans, Louisiana during the New Orleans school desegregation crisis of 1960. You've seen pictures of her being escorted by Federal Marshalls into school in front of large crowds of jeering grown-up racists. Just to give her a high-five would be cool. When you think about how traumatic the first day of school is for some five-year-olds, the fact that she didn't even cry is pretty astounding. Pairs well with Oprah, Rosa Parks, and Harriet Tubman.

Rosa Parks – Again, a big high-five here would be cool.

Betty Ford – She is surely a top choice of many Michiganders, many recovering alcoholics, and many First Lady scholars and First Lady aficionados. She raises an interesting question about whether whatever addictions one might have had while alive would carry over into the next life and into the dream dinner party arena. It would be awful to serve Betty Ford wine thinking her addiction had been ameliorated in the after-life, only to discover that you just caused a relapse.

Bill W. and Bob Smith – I suspect that many recovering alcoholics would like to have these two to dinner to thank them for conceptualizing the groundbreaking 12-step program Alcoholics Anonymous.

Hillary Rodham Clinton – History will treat this woman very kindly. She prompts feelings of both profound admiration and profound sympathy. And it turns out, she was right about everything she said about the man she beat in 2016.

Captains of Industry

For those whose religion is the accumulation of wealth, these guys are the Jesus and the Dalai Lama and the Gautama Buddha of money. In this case, telling them about the nature of wealth today and showing them what their philanthropic endeavors have wrought would be very gratifying. These guys frequently appear on applicant essays

Steve Jobs – I bet there are scores of Silicon Valley people for whom this guy is their Jesus.

Jack Welch – Not sure there's much else this guy could tell you other than what was in his book.

Henry Ford – This one had huge appeal for business leaders, historians, Detroit natives, and automobile aficionados. Not to mention, rabid anti-Semites.

Whitney Wolfe Heard – The woman who made Tindr, got kicked out of Tindr, so made Bumble would be a fascinating dinner guest.

Kylie Jenner – Many are quick to discount her business prowess. But I suspect she is quite knowledgeable.

Andrew Carnegie – There are a ton of Whartonny types who would invite him to a) show everyone how Whartonny they are and b) ostensibly try to learn tricks of how to be a captain of industry. I'm not a Whartonny type, but if you are, consider whether or not business has sufficiently changed such that any tricks of the trade Carnegie might provide would be obsolete. Then see John D. Rockefeller.

FUN FACT

Christopher Columbus was sort of a dipshit.

John D. Rockefeller – Same analysis as with Carnegie. But also, as with Carnegie, these guys were so generous and so philanthropic that the number of people who have benefitted from their generosity is likely infinite. I suspect some of those people—library goers, Carnegie-Mellon grads, foundation grant recipients—would like the chance to personally say thank you.
Bill Gates – Sure. But you can also just watch his TED talks.

Warren Buffet – See above. He'd give you advice, I'm sure, but other than that, what's the point?

Sam Walton – Ew. Though, taking him to a Wal-Mart would be fun. There's no way he buys that shit.

Elizabeth Holmes – She will likely be in prison, but if she can get a furlough to attend your dream dinner party, a frank discussion about how hype and greed can erode genius would make for very interesting dinner conversation. Also those fascinated by the riches to rags arc, could invite her along with Mike Tyson, Sammy Davis, Jr., O.J. Simpson, MC Hammer., Oscar Wilde, or Michael Jackson.

Sheryl Sandberg – I understand this, but why not just read her book?

Cornelius Vanderbilt – Vanderbilt University alumni could invite him to their dream dinner party and…sing the Vanderbilt fight song together?

Mark Zuckerberg – For his lackadaisical stance on the spread of misinformation, this guy just narrowly missed the villains list. Best of luck in 2022!!

Jeff Bezos – Again, because he makes $215,068,493 per day and pays his workers barely above minimum wage, this guy barely missed the villains list.

J.P. Morgan – See Carnegie and Rockefeller.

Sample dialogue:

Jeff Bezos: Anyway, as I was saying, I have a lot of money.

Mark Zuckerberg: Oh, same.

Warren Buffet: Right there with you, brother.

Jeff Bezos: Like, last night, my son called me and asked for 50 dollars

Mark Zuckerberg: Oh yeah?

Jeff Bezos: Yeah. And I said "50 dollars? I thought they discontinued the penny."

Warren Buffet: The same thing happened to me, but with 100 dollars

Mark Zuckerberg: Same

They sit silently. After a while:

Mark Zuckerberg: Fuck I'm so depressed

Jeff Bezos: I don't deserve any of this

Warren Buffett: All I've ever really earned is a regional golf tournament participation trophy. And a DUI

Jeff Bezos: My father never loved me

Mark Zuckerberg: My wife hates me

Warren Buffett: When I was five years old, I killed a polar bear with my hands

Mark Zuckerberg: What?

Warren Buffett: I was on one of my family's annual seal-clubbing expeditions. And my dad chained me to a polar bear and made me beat it to death with a snifter of cognac

Jeff Bezos: Oh my god

Warren Buffett: He said it'd 'make me a man.'

Mark Zuckerberg: Oh

Warren Buffett: Every time I shut my eyes, all I can picture is that polar bear's face. The blood. The guts. The cognac

Warren Buffett: Polar bear blood is different from regular blood. Thicker

Jeff Bezos: Um. The food is ready

Warren Buffett: Oh. Cool

Religions

Like Jesus, the thought here is that proximity to religious leaders will somehow result in their grace and sanctity and divine favor rubbing off on us. It's an interesting theory, but one that has yet to be proven. You also run the risk of pious people at your dream dinner party prohibiting the sort of mirth and merriment for which you yearn.

Gautama Buddha – Go for it.

Dalai Lama – I bet he'd be interesting. But no cursing, no slothfulness, no gluttony. How fun would it be?

Pope Francis – I like the idea of getting the pope to gossip about people. But the prospect of impromptu feet-washing frightens me. Proceed at your own risk.

Pope John Paul II – My wife is Polish. Every single person in her extended family has a photo of Pope John Paul II somewhere in their home. To them, this Pope as a dream dinner party guest accomplishes two things: celebrating national pride and ensuring a spot in heaven. Well played, Polish people. Well played.

St. Francis of Assisi – I'm into this. From what I understand, this guy was a wealthy man who gave up everything to live with animals and really found peace. Those who want to take their Marie Kondo to the next level would be well-advised to pick St. Francis's brain.

Virgin Mary – Same analysis as Jesus. But could be very disappointing. Like, what if she smokes? What if she tells you that she used all the Myrrh herself? And what do you even call her? "Pass the potatoes, Virgin Mary" just doesn't have the right ring to it.

St. Joseph -Same as Virgin Mary.

Martin Luther – This is the guy who posted those 98 things on the church door right?

The Scientists

While there are lots of smart people who took our scientific survey and who identified scientists and inventors as their top dream dinner party guests, this remains a highly niche category. And science is having a moment now that everyone is an armchair epidemiologist. Respondents who identified scientists as dream dinner party guests cited their eagerness to pay homage as the primary reason for doing so. I understand this. Just as a writer will be more apt to invite an author, a researcher or engineer or doctor will be more inclined to invite a scientist. Some of the individuals below have become cultural icons. But for some, inclusion into a person's dream dinner party means only one thing: questions about a particular area of study. Part of the appeal has got to be just showing the dream dinner party guest the advances that have occurred since he or she first delved into the area.

Albert Einstein – This is the crème de la crème of scientists, and one who would add that rare combination of luster and intellect to any dream dinner party. Einstein's brain was removed—without his family's permission—shortly after his death on Monday, April 18, 1955 by Dr. Thomas Harvey. Make sure he brings his brain to your dream dinner party if you invite him. Questions to ask: What does $e=mc^2$ even mean? Also, what is the deal with your hair?

Madam Curie – Lots of sciencey smart people with sciencey smart daughters wanted Marie Curie at their dream dinner party. Excellent choice. For those of you who don't know, Marie Curie was a physicist and chemist who conducted pioneering research on radioactivity.

Isaac Newton – Inviting this guy to a picnic in an apple orchard would be very fun and cool. Unless that whole apple falling on his head thing turns out to be bullshit. In that case, having a dream dinner party in an apple orchard would just be embarrassing.

Margaret Hamilton – There would not be a box with a list of men who walked on the moon without her.

Jane Goodall - Her work with chimpanzees has always fascinating. Her epiphany regarding chimpanzees' capacity for brutality was astonishing. A conversation with her about the things she has witnessed and how it informs her and our understanding of human beings would make for a very interesting dinner.

Galileo – This guy discovered that the earth was round. I think. Probably not even that fun. But you could play that song for him by Indigo Girls and that would kill a few minutes. And inviting him with Sir Isaac Newton, who has a cookie named after him, to discuss gravity by throwing food on the floor could be fun. Though would entail a great deal of clean-up at the end of the evening.

Thomas Edison – Invented the light bulb and the phonograph and motion pictures. You know, watching a movie with Thomas Edison would be pretty wild. Does not pair well with Dumbo the Elephant.

Jacques Cousteau – One question to ask people who lived a long time (this guy lived to be 87 and was diving and exploring the sea until his last day) is how did you live so long and so well? If you are into the sea and/or exploring it and/or conserving it, then you can do no better than this guy. He would pair nicely with other oceanic explorers of yesteryear.

Stephen Hawking – Interested in a dream diner party spent talking about theoretical physics and cosmology? This is your guy.

Charles Darwin – Watching this guy tear into someone (Sarah Palin) who believes that Adam and Eve roamed the earth with dinosaurs would be fun. But you'd be wasting a spot at your dream dinner party table on Sarah Palin. And do you really want to waste a spot on a spite guest?

Nikola Tesla – He was Serbian electrical engineer who helped design the modern alternating current. Plus, if you invite Elon Musk, then Tesla could drive around in a Tesla.

Rosalind Franklin - She spent three years studying X-ray techniques, returning to England to lead a research team to study the structure of DNA–all at a time when women weren't even allowed to eat in her college's cafeteria. Heading up another DNA research team was Maurice Wilkins, who ultimately betrayed Franklin when he showed scientists James Watson and Francis Crick, Franklin's ground-breaking X-ray image of DNA, known as Photo 51. Photo 51 enabled Watson, Crick and Wilkins to determine the structure of DNA. She went on to study the tobacco mosaic virus and polio, creating the foundation of modern virology, before passing away in 1958 at the age of 38. Watson, Crick and Wilkins won the Nobel Prize in 1962. Franklin's work was barely mentioned. Invite this bitch to your dream dinner party with a couple of these

Crick, Watson and Franklin fuckers and watch her kick some ass.

Nicolaus Copernicus – This is the guy who discovered that the sun, and not the earth, is the center of our solar system.

Alexander Graham Bell – Show this guy an iPhone, and his head would probably explode.

Aristotle – The Father of Western Philosophy. Anyone into philosophy would likely love to chat with Aristotle over dinner.

George Washington Carver – The most prominent black scientist of the 20th century and a leader in agricultural inventions and soil preservation. Pairs well with Neil DeGrasse Tyson.

Carl Sagan – Another cosmologist and astrophysicist for those into that sort of thing. Though, this guy also worked hard to popularize science.

Enrico Fermi – The "architect of the atomic bomb," he created the world's first nuclear reactor. Imagine watching HBO's *Chernobyl* with him after dinner. Or, since he died in 1954, show him the propaganda that emerged from the Cold War. Remember that movie *The Day After*? Man, how fucked up was that? Also, with a name like Enrico Fermi, I bet he loves Italian food.

J. Robert Oppenheimer – See Enrico Fermi. Except for the Italian food part.

Charles Darwin: I was invited here to discuss my research concerning the origin of the species.

Amy Comey-Barrett: *(reciting)* Our Father who art in heaven hallowed be thy name; forgive this Charles person for he knows not what he does.

They sit silently. After a while:

Adam and Eve: Fuck we are so hungry

Amy Comey-Barrett: *(reciting)* Our Father who art in heaven hallowed be thy name; forgive these people for they know not what they do

Adam and Eve: Bitch we're literally Adam and Eve

Charles Darwin: Fuck that bitch.

Adam and Eve: She sucks. Who wants Apple Brown Betty for dessert?

Charles Darwin: Wait – when you say that you're Adam and Eve, do you mean you're *that* Adam and Eve?

Adam and Eve: How many Adams and Eveses do you know? Especially ones who walk around and attend dinner parties naked?

Charles Darwin: Oh snap!

Explorers

The clear benefit to hosting an explorer is to ask him or her how it felt to see *x* for the first time. The danger, of course, is that he or she won't remember, or he or she will tell you that they were too intoxicated or that their syphilis created such hallucinations that they had no idea what they were discovering or otherwise unable to fully appreciate the moment at the time. Or that he or she wasn't even there! But then again, would Amelia Earhart's voyage really be that diminished if you found out that she had to be hammered for the whole trip? She might be a bad example, though, since you could also ask her where she died and then discover her remains and find great fame and fortune as the individual who discovered Amelia Earhart's remains! After dessert of course.

And, of course, did whomever discover Niagara Falls or the Puget Sound or the Mississippi River really *know* what they were discovering? And who really discovered Niagara Falls? Didn't the indigenous peoples who populated the land we now call the United States actually "discover" those things we deem to have been discovered?

The appeal of many, if not all, of these explorers identified as potential dream dinner party guests in our scientific poll is a geographic one. Someone who was born and lived in and revels in and studies the history of Seattle would be more apt and, in fact, encouraged to invite Peter Puget to his or her dream dinner party than someone who was born in and lived in and reveled in and studied North Carolina, who instead might be encouraged to invite Sir Walter Raleigh to his or dream dinner party.

The big downside to inviting an explorer to your dream dinner party is that so much of what they did has become de rigueur. Sure, the first time that Henry Hudson sailed up the Hudson River, I am sure it was a very big deal. But now millions of people call such a journey their "daily commute." I doubt Henry looked to his right and said, "That's going to be Manhattan someday—a land with magical Christmas window displays and street performers and great restaurants and the Yankees."

Christopher Columbus – Ew. Just no. What could he even contribute to the meal? He would probably sneak into the kitchen, steal a pie, and then claim it as his own.

Lewis and Clark – If these two can be one guest, and if you are into exploring or America or the wild western frontier, then this might be a good choice for you. Though both left journals, I do not think that in those days men talked about their feelings or vulnerabilities, and it could be nice to know: How did it *feel* to gaze upon the Rocky Mountains? How did it *feel* when Thomas Jefferson chose you to explore the Louisiana Purchase? Were you ever scared? What stood in the way of you and complete happiness?

Neil Armstrong – If you're into the moon, then a lengthy intimate visit with Neil Armstrong makes perfect sense. First, to meet the man who walked on the moon, and next, to interrogate him in great detail about how it felt and what he was thinking. Though, surely this must already exist somewhere, like in a memoir or something?

Daniel Boone – I just don't see this. Unless you're some sort of Kentucky person, then by all means have at it. If you are asking dream dinner party guests to bring a dish to pass, then be prepared for this one to bring some sort of freshly braised muskrat or rabbit or other rodent-like creature of some kind.

Henry Hudson – Dining with Henry Hudson at a fine Manhattan restaurant on the banks of the Hudson would be sort of magical. "Hey Henry, you did such a great job that they named this river after you!!" would definitely be cool.

Edmund Hillary – I wonder what Sir Edmund Hillary would think of the commodification of Everest. It would be interesting to dine with him there. And as stated above, dining with Mother Teresa and Sir Edmund Hillary at the top of Mt. Everest and watching Mother Teresa blow away would be fun.

EAT ME!

Charles Lindburger

This is that thing of when you host a dinner party and serve your guests little hamburger sliders, but then you steal them back before the guests can eat them.

Alexander the Great – I don't even know what this guy did, but it must have been great because that's literally his name, so invite him if you want. I don't care.

Amelia Earhart – She just barely missed our top ten. Her bravery gives her iconic status and makes her a hero for women. The mystery of her disappearance makes her a source of intrigue for people everywhere. People cited just wanting to meet her and get to know her as reasons for the dream dinner party invite. Identifying her as a potential dream dinner party guest also suggests that you, the host, via the associative property, have a brave and pioneering spirit. Also, cool jackets and accessories.

Charles Lindberg –HBO's *The Plot Against America* is giving Lindy a moment but likely not the sort of moment he'd like to be having. This one dropped in our poll and continues to drop as the scope and intensity of his anti-Semitism comes to light. But for a while, he was the most famous man in the world—for his courageous solo flight across the Atlantic and the fact that his baby got kidnapped.

Leif Erickson – I guess. If you are into Nordic warriors and whatnot.

Louis Hennepin – Popular in Minnesota.

Ferdinand Magellan – You're asking for trouble with this one. We know nothing about him except that he sailed around the world. Which I guess is a big deal; but then what?

Marco Polo – In addition to going swimming with him in the above-ground pool in your backyard and playing the stupidest game ever, you could discuss the intricacies of trading with China.

Peter Puget – This guy was an officer in England's royal navy who explored Puget Sound.

Sir Walter Raleigh – In addition to having his own brand of cigarettes, this guy did a bunch of exploring in and around the Carolinas.

Amelia Earhart: *(in an old fashioned bathing suit swimming around in your sketchy above-ground pool)* Marco!

Charles Lindberg: *(in an old fashioned bathing suit swimming around in your sketchy above-ground pool)* Polo!

Literally Marco Polo: Right here guys! Cannonball!! *(jumps in)*

Amelia Earhart: *(blindfolded and in an old fashioned bathing suit swimming around in your sketchy above-ground pool)* Marco!

Charles Lindberg: *(in an old fashioned bathing suit swimming around surreptitiously in your sketchy above-ground pool)* Polo!

Literally Marco Polo: Right here guys! What's going on?

Amelia Earhart: *(blindfolded and in an old fashioned bathing suit swimming around in your sketchy above-ground pool)* Marco!

Charles Lindberg: *(in an old fashioned bathing suit swimming around surreptitiously in your sketchy above-ground pool)* Polo!

Literally Marco Polo: Come one guys. This isn't funny.

Amelia Earhart: *(blindfolded and in an old fashioned bathing suit swimming around in your sketchy above-ground pool)* Marco!

Charles Lindberg: *(in an old fashioned bathing suit swimming around surreptitiously in your sketchy above-ground pool)* Polo!

Literally Marco Polo: Come on guys. What are you doing? This isn't funny.

Amelia Earhart: *(blindfolded and in an old fashioned bathing suit swimming around in your sketchy above-ground pool)* Marco!

Charles Lindberg: *(in an old fashioned bathing suit swimming around surreptitiously in your sketchy above-ground pool)* Polo!

Literally Marco Polo: I want to play too.

Amelia Earhart: *(blindfolded and in an old fashioned bathing suit swimming around in your sketchy above-ground pool)* Marco!

Charles Lindberg: *(in an old fashioned bathing suit swimming around surreptitiously in your sketchy above-ground pool)* Polo!

Literally Marco Polo: Just because I'm a famous Venetian merchant doesn't mean I don't have feelings you know!

Amelia Earhart: *(blindfolded and in an old fashioned bathing suit swimming around in your sketchy above-ground pool)* Marco!

Charles Lindberg: *(in an old fashioned bathing suit swimming around surreptitiously in your sketchy above-ground pool)* Polo!

Literally Marco Polo: Come on Chuck. Come on Millie.

Amelia Earhart: *(blindfolded and in an old fashioned bathing suit swimming around in your sketchy above-ground pool)* Marco!

Charles Lindberg: *(in an old fashioned bathing suit swimming around surreptitiously in your sketchy above-ground pool)* Polo!

Literally Marco Polo: Go ahead and have your fun. I'm going back inside.

Outliers

These potential guests defy categorization.

Adam and Eve – Once you get them some appropriate clothing, these two could be cool dinner party guests. Of course, you have to make sure they really existed. If you say, "I want to invite Adam and Eve to my dream dinner party," and *the* Adam and Eve you have in mind do not really exist, then it's possible that you would end up using two dream dinner party spots on Adam from accounting and Eve from book club. That would be a waste. But if they are real and really are the very first human beings ever, then you could basically solve many of the world's biggest mysteries—like does God exist and what does he or she sound like and how did things get created?

Cindy Crawford - Sometimes you just want to be surrounded by beautiful people, you know? Sometimes you just want a supermodel to feed you a grape, fan you, rub lotion on your body, wrestle with another supermodel in a giant vat of pudding, start a food fight, etc. Models are also advocates, storytellers, moguls, and pioneers. Many call Cindy the first "supermodel" which meant that for about a decade she was doing everything everywhere.

The Price is Right models (Janice, Dian, and Holly) – Anyone who has ever been sick and "forced" to stay home on a school day knows what great companions

Janice, Dian, and Holly can be. Invite them over and say thank you. Ask them stories about working with Bob Barker who could get quite handsy. And surely they are not there to work but maybe, if you ask nicely, Janice could hold a box of Rice-A-Roni for a few minutes while Holly hums the Cliffhanger game song and then when you win, Dian could let you sit in your car as you pretend to win it.

Paulina Porizkova – Paulina was the first central European to appear on *Sports Illustrated*'s swimsuit issue. She did that in 1984 at age 18. Lately, she has been a staple on Instagram telling her story about aging and grief.

Jacqueline Kennedy Onassis – She, the rare triple threat, barely missed our top 10. First, she would add class and sophistication to any dream dinner party. Second, she, notoriously private during her life, could open up and share insight—both substantive and emotional—from an era of intrigue. And third, a photograph with her would be a cherished keepsake for generations to come.

Harry Houdini – If you are into magic or just want to give your dream dinner party guests a thrill, then you can do no better than Houdini.

Anne Frank – Imagine telling this young girl that more than 30 million people speaking 70 languages have read, been enthralled by, been inspired by her diary. The Marlboro Man – Current cigarette smokers, long relegated to sidewalks, might revel in a symbol of the glory days of cigarette smoking as a dream dinner party guest. The Marlboro Man, retired by Philip Morris in 1998 after the master settlement between the cigarette companies and the attorneys general from all the states, symbolized smoking as rugged and manly and cool. Portrayed by a number of actors over the years, four of them died from smoking-related illnesses. If you do want the Marlboro Man at your dream dinner party, then be sure to specify which Marlboro Man you want.

Eunice Kennedy Shriver – She founded the Special Olympics and became a champion of children and people with intellectual disabilities. Frankly, I think one could select no finer a dream dinner party guest. Bonus: insight into growing up Kennedy.

Naomi Campbell – Another model turned businesswoman who also advocates for black models. "I never used to say the word racism; I just used to say, it's territorialism," she said. "I never wanted people to say that I used that as an excuse, that I was throwing that word out. Now I'm happy that everyone's all on the same page, that everyone feels comfortable to come out about their experiences without feeling some stigma. But for me, nothing's changed. I'm going to speak the same way."

Heidi Klum – She has always been an advocate for models with less conventional sizes and shapes. The show *Project Runway* made us cheer for fashion designers the same way we did for athletes.

Clara Peller – Those alive in the 1980s will recall an iconic Wendy's commercial where a lady looks at a burger from a fast food competitor and asks "Where's the beef?" That was Clara. The commercial became a cultural phenomenon, and that phrase became ubiquitous, used on t-shirts and bumper stickers and presidential debates. Advertising was inexplicably big in the 1980s and often news itself. The California Raisins were a thing. People collected Absolut Vodka ads. Nike launched "Just Do It." Pepsi and Coca Cola battled each other with musical commercials that had nothing to do with cola. Recall when Michael Jackson's hair caught on fire during the filming of a Pepsi ad. Max Headroom and Spuds McKenzie and Bartles and Jaymes were cool. And even Lou Reed pitched Honda.

Sample dialogue:

Janice: Thank god this is a sit-down dinner. I'm exhausted from standing near cars all day.

Dian: And pointing at them

Holly: Ugh. Pointing at cars is the worst

Janice: Couldn't agree more

Dian: We don't get paid enough for that shit

Janice: Bob Barker is worth 165 million dollars

Holly: Ha. And so fucking handsy. Last week I managed to spend my entire paycheck on the Uber home from work

Janice: I spent my entire paycheck at Quiznos

Dian: I donated my paycheck to the IDF

Holly: Jesus, Dian

Janice: We talked about this

Dian: Sorry

Holly: I don't know how much longer I can keep smiling like that

Janice: My face is numb all the time

Dian: I stopped smiling for 15 seconds on air last week

Holly: Yeah?

Dian: Yeah. And the execs at CBS took me aside and gave me these crazy new meds

Janice: What kind of meds?

Dian: I don't know, but I can run a 3 minute mile now. And whenever I close my eyes, I can literally hear the blood rushing through my veins

Holly: Sounds like meth

Dian: Man, you're probably right

The Villains

We sometimes can't help but love those we shouldn't. It's probably human nature. The other end of that continuum is that, when considering villains as potential dream dinner party guests, some of the appeal is wanting to physically harm them. But be prepared for any of these people to steal from you, snort coke in your bathroom, pass out in your bed, leave glitter in your carpet, and any other number of dream dinner party guest faux pas.

PRO TIP

Helen Keller hates Anne Frank and vice versa. Long story.

Hitler – He tops the list of villains. And astonishingly, he is near the top of the general list of dream dinner party guest invitees. When asked, nearly all respondents who identify him cite that they would want to kill him. But recall from our earlier analysis that this will not accomplish anything but soiling your linens. Those who think he has anything else to offer can shove this book up their ass.

Pol Pot – The second notable genocider on this list. If you are into the Khmer Rouge, the name popularly given to the followers of the Communist Party of Kampuchea and by extension to the regime through which the Communist Party of Kompuchea ruled in Cambodia between 1975 and 1979, then this is your man! Else that, I can't think of many more reasons to invite this man to your dream dinner party. Though it would be fun to serve chicken pot pie and then be able to say, "More pot pie, Pol Pot?"

Vladimir Putin – Imagine this one riding up to your house shirtless on horseback and then sauntering into your dream dinner party with his knee-high leather boots made from the hides of those of his comrades who dared double-cross him and sitting down and looking over your American cuisine—hamburgers and Freedom fries and milkshakes and apple pie and

PRO TIP

In the early 1960s, before he started his murderous cult, Charles Manson and Angela Lansbury were lovers. Do not invite them both to your dream dinner party, as it did not end well.

what not—with disdain and suspicion. Then when he leaves, you know that he bugged your whole house with surveillance equipment that can evade detection, and you know that you are living the rest of your life under Putin's watchful and disdainful eye.

Saddam Hussein – Though, I think his villainyness was overstated because of George W.'s daddy issues, he was still pretty awful.

Osama bin Laden – I know Barack Obama already killed him, but it would be fun to kill him again. But eating next to his corpse as flies buzz around him and rodents crawl in and out of his beard would not be so much fun.

Charles Manson – I think of this guy as one of those people whose infamy is far greater than it should be. Like, what did he ever really do except excel at getting attention? Make some exceptionally creepy prison art? I think we have seen all the discourse we need about this guy, but for those for whom he maintains some sort of fascination, this dream dinner party guest is perfectly adequate. Have fun, though, explaining his presence to your other dream dinner party attendees.

Joseph Stalin – This guy is often known merely as an adherent to Lenin's teachings and a proponent of communism, industrialization, and a profound love for Russia. But he was also a totalitarian ruler responsible for nearly a million executions and countless other deaths from terror and gulag camps and famine. So, let's say we put this in the "maybe" pile.

Kim Jong Il and/or Kim Jong Un – There's just no point here.

Donald J. Trump – Teasing him and watching him cry would be fun. He's the sort of bully who would cry easily. And that would be very gratifying. But fuck this guy. Fuck him and the dead fucking muskrat on his head and his orange epidermis and his too-long ties and his shitty shittiness.

Brett Kavanaugh – Invite this guy and tell him that it's a dry dinner party and watch his itty-bitty sphinctery fucking mouth shrivel into his stupid fucking rhombus head just before he starts to cry. Mock him as he pouts all dinner.

Newt Gingrich – A villain on many fronts—both politically and for the fact that he broke up with his dying wife while she was in the hospital. At a dinner

FAVORITE FOODS OF VILLAINS AND RUN-OF-THE-MILL SHITBAGS YOU MAY WISH TO INVITE:

- Richard M. Nixon: Cottage cheese
- Donald Trump: Peanuts; well-done steak; McDonald's Filet-O-Fish
- Vladimir Putin: Pistachio ice cream and beer
- Margaret Thatcher: Grilled Dover sole
- Idi Amin: Kentucky fried chicken and pizza
- Mao Zedong: Red-braised pork
- Adolf Hitler: Liver dumplings
- Joseph Stalin: Siberian nelma fish

party, he's the worst. This one time, he stayed up until 1 a.m. drinking Diet Coke, eating Twizzlers, and giggling like mad. The host gets to bed around 2 a.m., only to get woken up at 6 a.m. to the cat meowing. But the host doesn't have a cat. Turns out Newt Gingrich thought it'd be hilarious to crawl around the bedroom floor meowing at 6 in the morning.

Idi Amin – Hero or villain? You can ask him yourself!

Fidel Castro – The man at the epicenter of so much controversy could provide much insight into the communist incursion of the 1950s and 1960s. You could also ask him what he really thought of certain people and ideas, like, "what are the hurdles facing countries seeking to transition from a capitalist state dominated by foreign imperialism to a socialist society?" and "what was the deal with you and Barbara Walters?"

O.J. Simpson – Simple. Ask him if he did it. See what he says. You're, like, the best judge of character, right? Remember when your sister started dating Chad? You would totally be able to tell if OJ was telling the truth or not. Buffalo Bills football fans might be tempted to invite him, if they were assembling some sort of Buffalo Bills dream team dream dinner party. I bet he's also great at carving meats.

FOR ALL YOU PHILISTINES...

Top Real Life Mob Bosses:

- Semion Mogilevich
- Al Capone
- Charles "Lucky" Luciano
- Pablo Escobar
- John Gotti
- Carlo Gambino
- Frank Costello
- Meyer Lansky
- Vito Genovese
- Albert Anastasia
- Vincent Gigante
- Hisayuki Machii
- Tony "Big Tuna" Accardo
- Salvatore Riina
- Dawood Ibrahim
- Xie Caiping.

A Mob Boss – A risk-free, no-question-off-limits dinner with a real, live mob boss would be fascinating. We have a fascination teetering on love affair with these guys. Did they really leave guns hidden in bathrooms for mid-dinner Italian restaurant ambushes? Did anyone ever say, "leave the gun take the cannoli"? And more broadly, what is life like?

Richard Nixon – This guy has some renewed relevance insofar as he is being compared and contrasted with our 45th president. Certainly, one of the more complex villains.

Edward Snowden – To some, he's a patriot. To others, a villain. To others still, a heroic whistleblower. But mostly, he's a good old boy, never meanin' no harm, beats all you ever saw, been in trouble with the law since the day he was born.

Dick Cheney – Take him hunting! What could go wrong?

Lee Harvey Oswald – I can't think of another well-known figure that we know so little about. The proportion between his infamy and that which we know about him is highly skewed. Obviously, JFK assassination sleuths will want him there to ask him *the* question that is at the forefront of their minds. He has nothing to lose by telling the truth.

John Wilkes Booth – The other three-named presidential assassin. We sort of already know he did it, don't we? A Venn diagram of people who have confederate flags on the back of their trucks and people who would invite John Wilkes Booth to their dream dinner party is one solitary single shaded circle.

VI.   Nightmare Dinner Party

The latest thing is nightmare dinner parties. What's left to accomplish once your dream dinner party is complete? A nightmare dinner party, of course. This one's much easier. The goal here is to have as miserable a time as possible. If you could invite three people, living or dead, to your nightmare dinner party, who would it be?

The same thorough analysis should be expended on the nightmare dinner party as the dream inner party. Where to have it? What to serve? Décor? Music?

Imagine a dinner with Ivan the Terrible, Angelina Jolie's creepy incestuous brother from the 2000 Oscars, and Roseanne Barr at McDonald's while listening to country music. Nightmare.

But the real decision here is to whom to extend invites. To maximize the pain and suffering of a nightmare dinner party, we suggest inviting the following:

Tom Brady – Obviously. People outside of New England just do not like this guy (with the relatively recent exception of the fine residents of Tampa Bay). To paraphrase a popular New England mantra, they hate him because they ain't him. And they have a point. If he was on your favorite football team, you would love him, you would acknowledge him as the greatest quarterback of all time, you would begrudge him neither his beauty nor the beauty of his wife, literally a supermodel literally named "Giselle." Inviting Tom Brady to your nightmare dinner party accomplishes two things. First, he only eats steamed organic vegetables and one other thing that is like organic sprouts or something else organic. So, you would have to serve organic sprouts, and organic sprouts only which would truly make it a nightmare dinner party. Second, Tom Brady is so good looking that he would make everyone else feel ugly. So, as you sit there eating sprouts and drinking pure filtered water and feeling ugly you can say, "Ahhh. The perfect nightmare."

Gwyneth Paltrow – Obviously. For the same reasons identified above for Tom Brady, except no one—not even in New England—really likes her. You'd have to eat whole grain oat foods and wheat germy things, and you'd feel ugly. With Gwyneth, however, you also get the added nightmarish benefit of having to listen to her talk about yoga or jujitsu or her vaginal jade egg or her leech therapy or her tantric scrotum massage or her organic electrolysis methods, or whatever it is she is into.

Elon Musk – This guy is probably really annoying. And would also make you feel really bad about yourself because when was the last time you invented a car or became a billionaire or pioneered a space launch program for the people? Also, put him in the same room as Vladimir Putin and the two of them would likely hatch some sort of plot to take over the world.

Cardi B. / Post Malone – I just don't get it. People pay to hear them "sing?" Now I sound old.
Angelina Jolie's creepy incestuous brother James Haven – YouTube the 2000 Academy Award Ceremony for validation on this. Imagine looking up from the table as you lift a spoonful of tapioca pudding into your mouth and seeing him staring at you with his giant eyeballs and creepy lips and nose?

Roseanne Barr – This could push the nightmare dinner party into apocalypse dinner party territory. Stay away from her.

Appendix A

Favorite Foods of Potential Dream Dinner Party Guests

George Washington: Cherries

John Adams: Apple pan dowdy

Thomas Jefferson: Virginia sweet corn

James Madison: Virginia ham

James Monroe: Fried chicken with rice

John Quincy Adams: Fresh fruit

Andrew Jackson: Leather britches[1]

Martin Van Buren: Boar's head

William Henry Harrison: Hard cider

John Tyler: Grateful pudding

James Polk: Corn pone[2]

Zachary Taylor: Calas-Tous-Chauds[3]

Millard Fillmore: Beef stew

Franklin Pierce: New Hampshire fried pies

---

1   This was the name Andrew Jackson gave to green beans cooked with water and bacon, braised wild duck, wild goose, and fried apple pies.

2   This is a cornmeal cake softened with buttermilk and baked. Interestingly, Jacqueline Kennedy's nicknames for Lyndon and Lady Bird Johnson were "Uncle Corn Pone and his Li'l Porkchop."

3   "These delicious little cakes are great favorites in New Orleans with morning coffee, as indeed they were in the days of Zachary Taylor. Well acquainted with the Creole delicacies, he brought them back to Washington with him. Dissolve 1 yeast cake in 1/2 cup lukewarm water. When dissolved, stir into 2 cups cooked rice. Let rise overnight. Next morning, beat 2 eggs until light and lemony, add 4 tablespoons salt. Combine mixture and blend in 4 cups flour. Let dough rise 1 hour. Drop by tablespoons into deep fat that has been heated to a medium-hot temperature (360 degrees F.). Fry until browned lightly. Drain and serve piping hot, either with cane syrup or sprinkled with powdered sugar. Excellent either way. Makes 50 fritters." ---*President's Cookbook*, (p. 192-193)

James Buchanan: Moss rose cake

Abraham Lincoln: Honey

Andrew Johnson: Sweet potato everything

Ulysses S. Grant: Rice pudding

Rutherford B. Hayes: Angel cake

James Garfield: Squirrel soup

Chester A. Arthur: Macaroni pie with oysters

Benjamin Harrison: Presidential fig pudding

Grover Cleveland: Corned beef and cabbage

William McKinley: Hot lobster salad

Theodore Roosevelt: Coffee

William Howard Taft: Steak

Woodrow Wilson: Strawberry ice cream

Warren G. Harding: Chicken pot pie

Calvin Coolidge: Cornmeal muffins[4]

Herbert Hoover: Egg timbales

Franklin Delano Roosevelt: Lake Superior whitefish

Harry Truman: Fried chicken

Dwight D. Eisenhower: Old-fashioned beef stew

John F. Kennedy: New England fish chowder

Lyndon B. Johnson: Texas barbecue

Richard M. Nixon: Cottage cheese

Gerald Ford: Crab soup and homemade bread

Jimmy Carter: Baked grits with cheese

Ronald Reagan: Honey-baked apples[5]

4   Please call me if the thought of inviting Calvin Coolidge as one of your dream dinner party guests and serving him cornmeal muffins is something that you find intriguing.

George H. W. Bush: Corn pudding

Bill Clinton: Chicken enchiladas

George W. Bush: Huevos rancheros

Barack Obama: Black Forest Berry Honest Tea[6]

Donald Trump: Peanuts; well-done steak; McDonald's Filet-O-Fish

Vladimir Putin: Pistachio ice cream and beer

Grace Kelly: Cheeseburgers

Francois Hollande: Wine and hamburgers

Angela Merkel: Hungarian vegetable stew called "letcho" and meat and pickled vegetable soup called "solyanka"

Teresa May: Indian food

Pope Francis: Empanadas, sirloin steak, and dulce de leche

Justin Trudeau: Sushi

Shinzo Abe: Miso, rice, and natto

Dalai Lama: Bread, cheese, mushrooms, and cilantro

Benjamin Netanyahu: Pistachio ice cream

Narendra Modi: Khichdi (rice and lentils) and bhindi kadhi (buttermilk stew with okra)

David Cameron: Spicy sausage pasta

Mother Teresa: Fried locust with braised rodent and dirt sauce (probably)

Tony Blair: Fish and chips

Fidel Castro: Chef Erasmo Hernandez's vegetable soup

Nelson Mandela: Ox tripe, farm chicken, fermented milk, stuffed crabs, and

---

5   It would serve you well to have some jelly beans on hand should Reagan be on your dream dinner party guest list. Also, kick him in the dick when you see him. That fucker.

6   Obama also loves sea salt caramels and dark chocolate from Seattle chocolatier Fran's.

chicken curry.

Margaret Thatcher: Grilled Dover sole

Idi Amin: Kentucky fried chicken and pizza

Mohandis Gandhi: Brown rice and dal, locally-sourced seasonal vegetables, boiled beet root, and radishes

Mao Zedong: Red-braised pork

Adolf Hitler: Liver dumplings

Winston Churchill: Game, oysters, curry, and Stilton cheese

Joseph Stalin: Siberian nelma fish

George Orwell: Plum pudding

Agatha Christie: Devonshire cream

Jack Kerouac: Apple pie

J.D. Salinger: Roast beef[7]

Jean-Paul Sartre: Halva

Truman Capote: Italian summer pudding

Walt Whitman: Coffee cake

Sylvia Plath: Tomato soup cake[8]

7   Apparently, even recluses need to eat. Every Saturday evening, J.D. Salinger would travel from his secret home in Cornish, NH to Hartland, VT to attend the First Congregational Church's famous Saturday supper. Salinger would arrive early and write, and then help himself to the all-you-can-eat roast beef, mashed potatoes, and pie.

8   I was intrigued enough by this to Google it. Here is the recipe:

TOMATO SOUP CAKE À LA SYLVIA PLATH
2 CUPS SIFTED CAKE FLOUR
1 TBSP BAKING POWDER
1/2 TSP BAKING SODA
1/2 TSP GROUND CLOVES
1/2 TSP GROUND CINNAMON
1/2 TSP GROUND NUTMEG
1 CUP SEEDLESS RAISINS
1/2 CUP BUTTER
1 CUP SUGAR
2 LARGE EGGS
1 CAN (ABOUT 11 FLUID OUNCES) CONDENSED TOMATO SOUP

Willa Cather: Kolaches

John Steinbeck: Posole

F. Scott Fitzgerald: Turkey leftovers

Franz Kafka: Milk

Edgar Allen Poe: Eggnog

Ray Bradbury: Pizza soup

Georgia O'Keefe: Home grown vegetables and homemade yogurt (She lived to be 98, BTW.)

Pablo Picasso: Fish, vegetables, grapes, and rice pudding

Andy Warhol: A chocolate bar between two slices of bread and pre-made sandwiches from Automats (the vending machines that dispense sandwiches)

Ernest Hemingway: Hamburgers

Allen Ginsberg: Cold vegetarian borscht

Pearl S. Buck: Sweet and sour fish

1/2 CUP CHOPPED WALNUTS, OPTIONAL

PREHEAT THE OVEN TO 375F (190C/GAS MARK 5). GREASE AND FLOUR TWO EIGHT-INCH CAKE PANS.

SIFT THE FLOUR, BAKING POWDER, BAKING SODA AND SPICES TOGETHER. IN A SEPARATE BOWL, TOSS THE RAISINS WITH ABOUT A QUARTER CUP OF THE FLOUR MIXTURE AND SET ASIDE.

CREAM TOGETHER THE BUTTER AND SUGAR IN A MIXING BOWL UNTIL LIGHT, THEN BEAT IN THE WHOLE EGGS UNTIL THOROUGHLY MIXED.

TO THE CREAMED SUGAR/BUTTER MIXTURE, ADD THE FLOUR ALTERNATELY WITH THE SOUP BY THIRDS. FOLD IN THE RAISINS AND THE WALNUTS, IF USING.

DIVIDE THE MIXTURE EVENLY BETWEEN THE TWO CAKE PANS AND THEN BAKE FOR ABOUT 35 MINUTES, OR UNTIL A TOOTHPICK INSERTED IN THE CENTRE OF THE CAKE COMES OUT CLEAN ONCE REMOVED. LEAVE TO COOL IN THE PANS FOR FIVE MINUTES, THEN TRANSFER TO A CAKE RACK TO COOL THOROUGHLY. FROST WITH CREAM CHEESE FROSTING (BELOW).

CREAM CHEESE FROSTING

ILB CREAM CHEESE, AT ROOM TEMPERATURE

1/2 CUP BUTTER, AT ROOM TEMPERATURE

2 TSP VANILLA

I PINCH SALT

5 CUPS CONFECTIONER'S SUGAR

COMBINE THE CREAM CHEESE AND BUTTER IN A MIXING BOWL, AND BEAT TOGETHER UNTIL CREAMY AND UNIFORM. ADD THE VANILLA AND THE SALT, AND THEN GRADUALLY ADD THE CONFECTIONER'S SUGAR, BEATING UNTIL SMOOTH.

Friedrich Nietzsche: Lemon risotto

Harper Lee: Crackling bread

Beyonce: Whole wheat green pizza

Justin Timberlake: Linguini with lobster fra diavolo

Rihanna: Cauliflower and chicken curry

Alex Rodriguez: Maki and uramaki sushi rolls

Serena Williams: Microwave eggless molten lava cake

Oprah Winfrey: Baked gruyere mac and cheese with jalapenos

Emily Dickinson: Gingerbread

Edna St. Vincent Millay: Blueberry pie

Leo Tolstoy: Macaroni and cheese

Alice B. Toklas: Mushroom sandwiches

Bruce Springsteen: Not sure what his favorite food is. I would have guessed something nostalgic and fried and nostalgically fried from the Atlantic City boardwalk.

Hugh Jackman: Wine and cheese

Scarlett Johansson: Buffalo chicken wings

Justin Bieber: Spaghetti bolognese

Mariah Carey: Pizza

Britney Spears: Chocolate

Taylor Swift: She reportedly has too many favorites to count. The six staples that are always in her fridge are eggs, thinly sliced ham, thinly sliced chicken, orange juice, Diet Coke, Parmigiano-Reggiano cheese, and "some sort of binge food like a tube of cinnamon rolls or a giant tub of cookie dough."

Jennifer Aniston: Nachos

Kate Middleton: Sticky toffee pudding

Seth Meyers: Homemade Chex Mix

Dwayne "The Rock" Jonson: Braised sirloin tips

Katy Perry: Roasted blue foot mushrooms, vegetables, and apples

Appendix B

Favorite Drinks of Potential Dream Dinner Party Guests

Ben Franklin: Madeira (an oxidized and fortified wine)

Ernest Hemingway: Mojito (Obviously. Anyone who identified Ernest Hemingway as their dream dinner party guest would surely already know to serve mojitos.)

F. Scott Fitzgerald: Gin Rickey

Truman Capote: Screwdriver

Jack Kerouac: Margarita

Humphrey Bogart: Scotch

James Bond: Martini

Winston Churchill: Whiskey and water

Jeff Lebowski: White Russian

Pablo Picasso: Absinthe[9]

Barack Obama: Bud Light (elitist)

Beyonce: Long Island iced tea

Bono: Jack Daniels

Gisele Bunchen: Peach passion

Chevy Chase: Piña colada

George Clooney: Raspberry cheesecake

Johnny Depp: Blueberry-ginger bourbon sour

Mike Ditka: Cape Cod

---

9   I have always wondered what this is and so I just Googled it. According to Wikipedia, it is "an anise-flavoured spirit derived from botanicals, including the flowers and leaves of Artemisia absinthium ('grand wormwood'), together with green anise, sweet fennel, and other medicinal and culinary herbs. *Absinthe* traditionally has a natural green colour, but may also be colourless." Absinthe has often been portrayed as a dangerously addictive psychoactive drug and hallucinogen. The chemical compound thujone, which is present in the spirit in trace amounts, was blamed for its alleged harmful effects. By 1915, absinthe had been banned in the United States and in much of Europe, including France, the Netherlands, Belgium, Switzerland, and Austria–Hungary, yet it has not been demonstrated to be any more dangerous than ordinary spirits.

Clint Eastwood: Red wine – Cabernet

Will Ferrell: Corona

Lady Gaga: Jameson on the rocks

Paris Hilton: Tequila

Hulk Hogan: Piña colada

Scarlett Johansson: Champagne

Angelina Jolie: Tequila

Richard Nixon: Chateau Lafite Rothschild

Gerald Ford: Martinis

Ronald Reagan: Orange blossom special

William Clinton: Snakebite

Spike Lee: Absolut Vodka

Madonna: Pomegranate martini

Matthew McConaughey: Miller Lite

Cal Ripken, Jr.: Rum runner

Julia Roberts: Scorpino

J.K. Rowling: Gin and tonic

Slash: Jack Daniels

Sting: Jack Daniels

Taylor Swift: Whiskey sour

John Travolta: Bombay Sapphire martini

Oprah Winfrey: Lemon drop martini

George Washington: Dark porter laced with molasses

John Adams: Drank a glass of hard cider every morning; then drank porter, rum, and Madeira all day

Thomas Jefferson: Wine

James Madison: Champagne

James Monroe: Burgundy

Abraham Lincoln: Rarely drank

Grover Cleveland: Beer

Theodore Roosevelt: Mint juleps

Franklin Delano Roosevelt: Gin martini

Harry Truman: Old fashioned

John F. Kennedy: Daiquiris, Bloody Marys, and Heineken beer

Appendix C

Allergies of Potential Dream Dinner Party Guests

George Washington: Ragweed, pollens, dust, grass, trees

Andrew Jackson: Molds, poultry

James Buchanan: Dogs, cats, insect bites

Grover Cleveland: Animal hair, chocolate, soap, wood, fish, dust

Woodrow Wilson: Dairy products

Calvin Coolidge: Egg yolks, milk, house dust[10], tobacco, chives, wheat, insect bites, cosmetics

Lyndon Johnson: Chocolate, wool, penicillin, fish

Scarlett Johansson: Grass pollen

Serena Williams: Peanuts

Bill Hader: Peanuts

Malia Obama: Peanuts

Drew Barrymore: Garlic

Clay Aiken: Tree nuts

Britney Spears: Bee stings

Billy Bob Thornton: Shellfish

John F. Kennedy: Dogs, dust, horses

Theodore Roosevelt: Hay fever

Drew Brees: Gluten

Lionel Ritchie: Dairy

Jon Bon Jovi: Hay fever

Kate Middleton: Horses

Cameron Diaz: Flowers

---

10   If you are thinking, "Oh my gosh, if I invite Calvin Coolidge to my dream diner party, then I have to make sure my house is dust-free," let me assure you that you have bigger problems than keeping a clean house if Calvin Coolidge is one of your potential dream dinner party guests. Ew. Just ew.

Tiger Woods: Pollen

Miley Cyrus: Cinnamon

Beyonce: Perfume

Halle Berry: Shellfish

Ariana Grande: Cats, bananas, shellfish

Appendix D

Ways to Say What Teen Boys Did Underneath Their Iconic Red Bathing Suited Farrah Fawcett Mexican Blanket Poster

Shaking hands with the milkman

Poaching the egg

Manual override

Marching the penguin

Double clicking

Polishing the banister

Petting the cat

Lone Rangering

Boxing the one-eyed champ

Celebrating Palm Sunday

Visiting the safety deposit box

Finding Nemo

Cuffing the carrot

Cooking cucumbers

Dialing the rotary phone

Making waffles

Doing a Meg Ryan

Turning on the sprinklers

Shucking the corn

Softening the peach

Spearing the bearded clam

Dating Pamela Handerson

Beating the Bishop

Bopping the baloney

Choking the chicken

Paddling the pink canoe

Scratching Yoda behind the ears

Basting the ham

Battling the purple headed yogurt slinger

Taking selfies at the Bean

Flogging the dolphin

Going to the palm prom

Holding your sausage hostage

Jerking the gherkin

Dotting the "I"

Burping the worm

Tapping into your potential

Petting the poodle

Pumping the keg

Playing closet frisbee

Combing the hair on your bald pig Sally

Playing couch hockey for one

Cuddling the kielbasa

Fastening the chin strap on the helmet of love

Flipping your omelet

Galloping the lizard

Going Han Solo on your Millennium Falcon

Looking for clues with Fred and Daphne

Making the bald man puke

Making a cash withdrawal

Making instant pudding

Making chowder with Sailor Ned

Mangling the midget

Punching the clown

Punching the munchkin

Sailing the mayonnaise seas

Shaking hands with Lincoln

Shaking hands with Dr. Winky

Teaching the snake to Lambada

Tenderizing the tube steak

Waxing the Buick

Taking your talents to South Beach

Auditioning the finger puppets

Badgering the witness

Making soup

Preparing the monologue

Giving Rosie the lifeboat (a *Titanic* reference)

Clicking the home page

Drilling for oil

Boxing with Richard

Buffing the banana

Buttering the corn

Cleaning your rifle

Washing the meat

Wiggling the walrus

Wrestling the eel

Roughing up the suspect

Rubbing Rob Reiner

Adjusting the antenna

Aiding and abetting the felon

Giving yourself a hand

Rotating the drive head

Keynoting in Cupertino

Appendix E

Taco Eating Methods

Angelina Jolieing – This is when you eat tacos with your brother and your brother has some guacamole on the side of his mouth and you lick it off for him.

The Bjork – This is when you bite into a taco, and it's so great that you shriek in a unique, somersaulting, and whimsical soprano.

Boo Radleying – This is when you eschew guacamole in your taco, and instead you whittle fun little sculptures out of the avocados and leave them in the tree for the neighborhood children.

Calvin Kleining – This is when there's a disproportionate amount of meat in your taco, and you say, "Look at all of this meat!"

Charlie and the Chocolate Factorying – This is when you have four grandparents recuperating in one bed in your living room and they ask you to run out and get some Epsom salts and while you are out you stop at Chipotle.

Descartes – This is when you think, "This is a great taco," when you are eating your taco.

Eiffel's Lament – This is when you remove the meat from your taco and make a tower out of it and then eat it later.

The Eileen Fischer – This is when you're an older woman and you drape a simple cotton napkin, an earth tone hued napkin, on your lap before you start to eat your taco.

Eleanor Rigbying – This is when you pick up the rice at a church where a wedding has been and you take the rice home, put some cilantro in it, and then put the rice in a taco.

Grey Gardening – This is when you feed tacos to your feral cats and eat corn right out of the can.

Gwen Stefaniing – This is when you put the whole taco in your mouth, and your mouth is so full that you don't speak.

Henri Matisse – This is when you get a packet of hot sauce, and you artfully dribble it onto the taco.

The John Deere – This is when you make lawn mower sounds when you are eating your taco.

Janet Jacksoning - This is when whomever made your taco slides it through a puddle of wayward sour cream and you say, "Nasty!" but rather than send it back, you wipe off the sour cream, but you can still mentally taste it.

The Jason Wu – This is when you're at an inaugural ball and eating tacos, and everyone's like, "Tacos?!"

The JD Salinger – This is when you eat tacos all by yourself in your cabin and then someone stops by, and you say, "Get away from my tacos!"

Karen Carpentering – This is when you politely refuse a second taco and while everyone else is finishing their meal, you stand up and sing a song in a voice so rich and creamy and smooth that it feels like you're standing underneath a waterfall of rich creamy queso blanco.

Louis Vuittoning – This is when you put your initials on your taco.

Naomi Campbell – This is when you throw your taco at somebody, but then you are still hungry, so when that person leaves the table, you reassemble the taco you just threw and eat it.

The Narciso Rodriguez - This is when you eat a taco in Grant Park in Chicago after your husband gets elected.

Poseidon's March – This is when you eat fish taco longitudinally, beginning at the base and proceeding counter-clockwise.

The Renault – This is when you make engine sounds when you are eating your taco.

Rihannaing – this is when you get a taco at a taco truck and it starts to rain so you have to eat your taco one-handed since you have to hold an umbrella with your other hand

The Savory Beaver - – This is when you gnaw a hole in the base of the taco and extract the meat through it.

The Smith Corona – This is when you eat your taco from left to write and when you reach the end of the taco, you make an audible "ding" sound and then restart eating the taco on the left.

The Ted Kaczynski – This is when you eat tacos all by yourself in your cabin while you compose a manifesto.

Troitsky Line – This is when you mentally divide a taco into two hemispheres and then proceed to eat the left hemisphere first.

Zwischenzug – [from the German "in-between move"] This is when you order a plate of three tacos and you forget how many you've eaten and you think you might be on your third, but then you look at your plate and you see a taco remaining and you are very elated because you really want another taco

Appendix F

What Your Favorite Pizza Topping Says About You

Pepperoni - Whenever you turn the volume on your TV up or down, it has to land on an even number.

Sausage – Once, you were on a boat, trolling for yellowtail amidst a school of dolphin about 4 miles off San Diego. Dolphin are too smart to take lures, aren't shy near small boats, and feed on the same bait schools as yellowtail and tuna, so it's strategic to follow them). As if cued, all ~50-75 dolphins simultaneously stopped jumping and disappeared into the depths for about 30 seconds. Immediate, unnerving quiet. With great fanfare, they all suddenly burst out of the water in a near-perfect row about a football field wide, and for a while, synchronized jumps ahead of our boat. Then they were gone.

Bell peppers – You and your dad once witnessed a white figure fly across your backyard in 1999. It didn't have arms or legs or a face, it was basically like a sheet, and it flew across the yard at superhuman speed.

Pineapple - You've noticed recently that you are very attracted to people with buggy eyes, or what your friend likes to call frog-features.

Meatballs – You have put a nicotine patch on someone after sleeping with them in an effort to get him or her addicted to you.

Bacon – You can't decide what kind of patio furniture to buy.

Anchovies – You love wearing white shirts with black pants so much that you don't even mind when you walk into a restaurant and people start giving you their orders.

Black olives – You once threw your iPhone out the window when Words with Friends wouldn't accept the word "uploader" in a game and you could have had 179 points.

Spinach – You once made a 176 song Spotify playlist, and when you played it on shuffle, it played two Journey songs in a row, which made the randomness not feel very random and thus diminished the luster of your new playlist, so you deleted it.

Broccoli – The porn that you are into is very niche, and you have exhausted the world's supply of it in just under eight months.

Hot peppers – During quarantine, you accidentally shaved a stripe in the back of your head while trying to cut your own hair.

Cherry tomatoes – Your spouse has made you sick by using expired food in a recipe he or she was making.

Basil – You have asked your housekeeper not to talk to your Alexa.

Eggplant – You once flew to London to see Adele perform in concert, only to have Adele cancel the show that very day due to vocal strain.

Sun-dried tomatoes – Your hand lotion works so well that you find it difficult to take notes on your iPad Pro.

Porcini mushrooms – Once, while driving from Cancun to Merida at night, you swerved to avoid a huge pothole in the middle of the road. About 200 meters ahead, you notice a car has got its hazard lights on parked on the side of the road, so you decided to stop and check to see if they needed help (you thought it might have been a flat tire). You parked, approached the car, and as you got closer, you saw what appeared to be two passengers in the back. There was no one in the driver seat, and those two figures you had seen were mannequins with wigs and faces drawn with a marker.

Ham - Your grandpa had a good relationship with the deer who lived around him. In the final minutes of his life, dozens of deer all visited his house and stood outside. As soon as he passed, they left. That had never happened before, not in those numbers.

Onions – You came out of a store one day and turned the corner to see a crow trying to read a paperback novel on a park bench. He was perched on the bench, turning pages with his beak. When he noticed you staring, he hopped away like you caught him red-handed and took flight a moment later. You ended up getting a tattoo of a crow reading a book because the incident left such an impression on you. No one really seems to believe you, but dude, corvids are fucking *smart*.

Extra mozzarella – In college, you painted your window black except for two peepholes for binoculars, so you could spy on people in the quad.

Blue cheese – You went to a wilderness survival school, and there was this guy there named Charlie who never wore a shirt, rode this really beat-up motorcycle everywhere, and mined Bitcoin for a living. He didn't bring a tent, so he slept on a tarp on the ground for the whole week and ate canned beans even though the camp provided meals. He cried a lot and hugged everyone at the end of the week.

Chicken - In the eighth grade, you had a substitute teacher named Uncle Cliff. You forget his real name, but he said everyone called him Uncle Cliff. Instead of teaching English for the day, he just spoke about his life. He said he was a self-proclaimed renaissance man. And by his presentation (which he started showing off from the classroom tv), it looked like it. From what you can remember, he used to be a high school teacher for a long time, and later became a tech engineer for NASA and then Apple. He also played for the 49ers in the 60s/70s and was a member of the Knights Templar.

Kalamata olives – You have thought about having some of your vocal cords removed so you sound more like Betty Boop.

Snow peas – There's a guy in your hometown named Bam Bam Bigelow who feeds the ducks all day.

Prosciutto – You are a marine biologist and once met someone on Craigslist who was giving away a sea lion.

Wild mushrooms – You met your bandmate when you ordered food from him at the Taco Bell drive-thru. Things were great for a while—you even played a few shows in Austin together—but the band broke up when you discovered your bandmate, the one you met at the Taco Bell drive-thru, was in another band when you saw that band's rock opera on You Tube

Prawns – Your great-aunt Renata wanted to move to America but didn't know how, so she let an American GI impregnate her.

Jalapeño peppers – Your aunt was hitting on your fiancé at your grandmother's funeral.

Ricotta cheese – The homeless man who sits outside your local McDonald's tells erectile dysfunction jokes, and sometimes you can't help but laugh at them.

Beans – Once, while staying at a youth hostel in Tel Aviv, you went out to lunch with some people staying at the hostel with you, and while you were at lunch, a random man sat down at your table and started eating your French fries.

Portobella mushrooms – There is an Asian man who walks around the Chicago neighborhood where you live; he is always smoking cigarettes with one of those long fancy cigarette holders and has a Nalgene bottle filled with an odd blue liquid attached to his belt.

Acknowledgments

I hereby acknowledge all the folks who ruminated on, identified, shared, discussed, analyzed, and otherwise considered their selections for their dream dinner party. It has been so much fun considering and debating these with so many. I would also like to acknowledge my family for their perpetual patience and good humor. Acknowledgements for the Humorist Media interns, Zoë Appelbaum and Lily Emalfarb and who shepherded this book from inception to publication. I acknowledge Andy Newton for his unparalleled editorial skills, encouragement, and good humor. I acknowledge Ross Bullen, my co-host at the Official Dream Dinner Party Podcast for his enthusiasm for the dream dinner party. Lastly, I am not sure how I became a mere marionette in the Marty Dundics's Machiavellian puppet show that is Humorist Media. But I am so glad I did. His tenacity, fearlessness, and heart are all such huge sources of inspiration which need to be acknowledged. I officially acknowledge Marty.

About The Author

Gary M. Almeter is the author of the memoir *The Emperor of Ice-Cream*, the novel *Kissing the Roadkill Back to Life*, and co-editor with Rafael Alvarez of *A Lovely Place, A Fighting Place, a Charmer: The Baltimore Anthology*. Gary is an attorney who lives in a quaint and cozy neighborhood in Baltimore, MD with his wife, three children and dogs, Dave and Mixly. His short stories, essays and humor pieces have appeared in *McSweeney's, Writer's Bone, Weekly Humorist, 1966,* and *Splitsider*. He's been dreaming about his dream dinner party for decades.